Critical acclaim for

MENTORING BEYOND AI

"*Mentoring Beyond AI* equips readers with the tools and insights needed to embark on their own mentoring journey. From setting the stage and understanding the nuances of mentorship to cultivating a mentoring mindset and building character, each chapter serves as a beacon of guidance in an increasingly complex world."

— Jose M. Hernandez, former NASA Astronaut
and author of *Reaching for the Stars*

"Through a rich tapestry of history, practical insights, and visionary foresights, this book serves as both a compass and a roadmap for mentors and mentees navigating the complexities of modern learning and development.... This book does a great job addressing the art of mentoring in the digital age, making it an indispensable guide for anyone looking to leave a lasting impact in their protégés' lives amidst the ever-evolving technological landscape."

— Juan Hurtado, CEO, Impetuh LLC and former
Director of Science, Technology and Innovation
U.S. Southern Command

"From a title that presents domains that may seem worlds apart, this work could serve as a textbook for rising above the levels of lecturer, teacher, educator, motivator, coach, trainer, and philosopher into a comprehensive, integrated model for inspirational mentoring."

— Steve Fritts
Adjunct Professor of business & technology

"I began reading this book rather confused as to the role of a mentor versus a teacher or apprenticeship. I have many years of experience teaching and precepting students and new employees, but rarely viewed myself as a mentor. This book has made me reevaluate my position on mentoring, and provided useful steps and information to become a better mentor."

— Monica Ponce
Registered Nurse and former Paramedic

"In a world racing towards automation and artificial intelligence, *Mentoring Beyond AI* emerges as a vital reminder of the irreplaceable value of human touch in mentorship and leadership. The insights within these pages are profound, drawn from a deep well of real-life experience and a heartfelt understanding of what truly motivates and inspires people. A seminal work that redefines the contours of effective leadership in the 21st century."

— Alejandro Ortiz
Food & Beverage Development Manager/Chef

MENTORING
BEYOND AI

FIRST EDITION

Forging Pioneers
for the Dawning Era of
Artificial Intelligence,
the Metaverse, and Space

Jerry F. Miller, PhD
Anitha Kurup, PhD
S. Sitharama Iyengar, PhD
Naveen Chaudhary, PhD
Niki Pissinou, PhD

Quest Publishing ❖ *Miami, Florida*

Inquiries should be directed to :

Quest Publishing
2655 S. Le Jeune Road, Suite 500
Miami, FL 33134 U.S.A.
Tel. +1 305.779.3069 • Fax +1 305.901.2120
email: editor@quest-publishing.com

ISBN-13: 978-0-9769416-6-8
Library of Congress Control Number 2024906027

Chief Editor: Jacques Island
Copy Editor: Beth Klein
Assistant Editor: Krizza Quintos
Graphics: Lucia Toro & Peachy de Mesa

First Edition: March 2024

10 9 8 7 6 5 4 3 2 1

Cover designed from images by
yongheng19962008/stock.adobe.com and Harvinder/stock.adobe.com.
This book follows the guidelines of the Modern Language Association
(MLA9) for citations and formatting, with some exceptions for abbreviations.
It is distributed 'as is' without warranty. While the authors believe all information contained herein is accurate, nothing in it constitutes a legal opinion,
or financial or psychological advice. Neither the authors nor the publisher
shall have any liability with respect to information in this book. Further,
neither the authors nor the publisher have any control over or assume any
responsibility for websites or external resources referenced in this book.

Visit us on the web at quest-publishing.com

Contents

Contributor Anecdotes

Anecdotes presented in this book as sidebars are contributions from mentors and mentees about their positive and negative experiences. They serve to highlight some of the mentoring "lessons" in this book's chapters, but they are also useful in their own right. Readers may want to go directly to these anecdotes for their value as abbreviated "cases in point."

Figures

Dedication

From numbers to dreams . . .

This book is dedicated to Srinivasa Ramanujan (22 December 1887 to 26 April 1920), one of the finest mathematicians and autodidacts to have ever lived.

More importantly, this work is also dedicated to the living minds who are destined to surpass Ramanujan, and to the mentors who give unselfishly of their time to identify and help them achieve the new discoveries we now only dream about or have yet to conceive, and move the human condition beyond our immediate AI horizon.

Acknowledgements

We wish to acknowledge the influences of Dr. Vyas and Dr. Baldev Raj, who inspired and mentored us on our first steps in this effort. This book might never have come to fruition without their initial encouragement and guidance.

Additionally, the authors wish to thank the following individuals, in order of appearance, for contributing mentoring anecdotes: Joel Rodriguez, Baldev Raj, Edda Rivera, K. V. Dinesha, Sanghamitra Bandyopadhyay, Beth Klein, Amaresh Chakrabarti. Madhusoodan Hosur, Elizabeth Gonzalez, Hina Gokhale, Anitha Kurup, M. S. Valiathan, Nalin Surie, R. A. Mashelkar, V. S. Ramamurthy, and Bikramjit Basu.

We also need to note that some of the research included in this book was sponsored by the *Army Research Office* and was accomplished under Grant Number W911NF-21-1-0264.

The views and conclusions contained in this document are those of the authors and should not be interpreted as representing the official policies, either expressed or implied, of the Army Research Office or the U.S. Government.

Foreword

. . . from dreams to the stars

Mentoring is the timeless art of guidance and wisdom passed down through generations, shaping lives, careers, and even entire civilizations. It is the beacon that illuminates the path to success, casting light on the darkest of uncertainties.

In *Mentoring Beyond AI*, the authors embark on a journey that transcends the boundaries of time and technology, exploring the profound impact of mentoring in an era dominated by artificial intelligence.

My own odyssey, from a restless child to a NASA astronaut, has been interwoven with the guiding hands of mentors who believed in my potential even when I struggled to see it myself.

Source: National Aeronautics and Space Administration (NASA) - http://spaceflight.nasa.gov/gallery/images/shuttle/sts-128/html/jsc2009e082549.html, Public Domain, https://commons.wikimedia.org/w/index.php?curid=7589018

It began in second grade, when a compassionate teacher, Ms. Young, recognizing the turmoil caused by my family's frequent relocations, advocated for stability, urging my parents to settle in Stockton, California. This pivotal moment laid the foundation for the stability and support that would shape my future.

When I confided in my father about my dream of becoming an astronaut, he bestowed upon me a recipe for success—a simple yet profound blueprint consisting of five essential ingredients. The first of which was, "Determine your purpose in life," he said, igniting a flame of ambition within me. With each rejection letter from NASA—eleven in total—I revisited his words, reminding myself of the roadmap he had entrusted to me. Through determination, preparation, and an unwavering work ethic, I persevered, eventually earning the privilege of donning the iconic blue NASA flight suit.

As I reflect on my journey, I realize that my story is not just one of personal triumph, but a testament to the transformative power of mentoring. It is this realization that fuels the pages of *Mentoring Beyond AI*, a comprehensive exploration of mentoring's evolution through the ages and its enduring relevance in an era defined by rapid technological advancement.

In the opening chapters, the authors journey through history, tracing the symbiotic relationship between mentoring and technological progress. From the dawn of civilization to the emergence of artificial intelligence, mentors have served as custodians of knowledge, guiding humanity through the tumultuous currents of change. Drawing inspiration from luminaries such as Srinivasa Ramanujan, we glean insights into the timeless principles that underpin effective mentoring.

As we delve deeper, *Mentoring Beyond AI* equips readers with the tools and insights needed to embark on their own mentoring journey. From setting the stage and understanding the nuances of mentorship to cultivating a mentoring mindset and building character, each chapter serves as a beacon of guidance in an increasingly complex world.

Yet, the true essence of mentoring lies not in imparting knowledge, but in fostering a sense of community and camaraderie. Through case studies and real-world examples, we witness the transformative power of mentoring in action, from nurturing gifted protégés to navigating the challenges of an AI-driven world.

In the final chapters, the authors expertly peer into the future, where virtual realms and outer space converge to redefine the boundaries of mentorship. As we stand on the precipice of a new era, *Mentoring Beyond AI* offers a roadmap for navigating the uncharted territories ahead, where human ingenuity and technological innovation intertwine in unprecedented ways.

As I pen these words, I am reminded of the countless mentors who have shaped my own journey—the teachers, family members, and colleagues who believed in me when I faltered, and guided me through the darkest of nights. *It is to them that I dedicate this foreword*, as a tribute to their unwavering belief in the power of mentoring to transcend barriers and transform lives.

In closing, I invite you to embark on this journey with an open heart and a curious mind, for in the pages of *Mentoring Beyond AI* you will find not just a roadmap to success but a celebration of the human spirit and the enduring power of mentorship to light the way forward.

JOSE M. HERNANDEZ
Former NASA Astronaut
Tierra Luna Engineering CEO
University of California Regent
Author of *Reaching for the Stars*
Subject of *A Million Miles Away* movie

Editor's Note

Nearly everything we invent or make requires logic, reasoning, and the use of the hard sciences. Just getting a book to a reader's hands requires design calculations to fit words into the right spaces. And designing a space ship ... is a bit more complicated. But both, and almost everything else we do, involve numbers and problem solving whether we are conscious of the process or not.

We are now in the age of fast-paced information and high technology advancements: the age of *artificial intelligence* and the coming *metaverse*. Now is more imperative than ever to build upon the collective achievements and wisdom of others who have come before us rather than "reinvent the wheel"—and that is what mentoring is about.

This book is for those of us who may be seeking mentors, new mentors who are just getting started on the road to the rewarding world of mentoring, and those established in the mentoring process who may want to refresh their skills in establishing strong mentoring relationships.

Essentially, within these covers there is something for everyone in the process of learning and innovating. It provides a guideline for establishing or reinforcing a successful mentoring program using effective intervention strategies, and it can be used in schools, the workplace, and within communities at large.

Traditional mentoring provides guidance and intellectual support to young people who need guidance in a wide array of areas. This book expands the concept of mentoring by shifting the focus from addressing only current needs, to building and nurturing mentor-protégé relationships throughout one's lifetime.

Literature in the field shows that youth mentoring expands from a relatively small intervention to cornerstone services that can be implemented through worldwide mechanisms across institutions. This book offers a comprehensive overview of successful mentoring programs and points the way toward new ideas in inter-disciplinarity and cross-cultural mentoring. More importantly, it does so from an international perspective, transcending backgrounds, moving across cultures, and facilitating cross-pollination of ideas to provide a global mentoring movement.

In this, we attempt to draw critical elements from current mentoring, providing refreshing new perspectives, and proposing new global mentoring models for the new line of doers to thrive in the age of artificial intelligence, the metaverse, and the newest frontier that is space exploration.

Jacques Island
Chief Editor

P A R T

I

Mentoring in the Age of AI

This section provides an overview of mentoring through the ages and today, including:

- the history of mentoring,

- the fundamentals of the mentoring process, and

- an understanding that technology will play a critical role in the future of mentoring.

CHAPTER

1

Mentoring and Technology Over the Ages

Yet taught by time, my heart has learned to glow
for others' good, and melt at others' woe.

—Homer

MENTORING IS AS old as human history. It has evolved along the way but primarily remains a process of human interaction, depending foremost upon building a relationship between mentor and protégé. This essential element has remained unchanged for centuries.

Mentoring as we know it today can be traced back to its roots in ancient Greek mythology, through the story of Odysseus. We learn from Homer's epic poem, *Odyssey*, that Odysseus, then the king of Ithaca upon being called to fight the Trojan War, entrusted his son Telemachus' education to his lifelong friend, Mentor. Odysseus asked Mentor to be his son's "teacher, adult friend, counselor, and protector." From this entrusted relationship springs our modern definition of "mentoring," or guiding someone in the attainment of their goals.

In "Who Exactly was Mentor?" Jean Rhodes writes that in Homer's *Odyssey* the guide Mentor starts Telemachus on his mentoring journey, but it is through the Greek goddess Palle Athene (Athena) who in the forms of a shepherd, a seagull, a ship captain's daughter, and a swallow, in addition to "a Taphian chieftain named Mentes," was the main mentor for Telemachus. Rhodes contends that using these guises, Athena became a "credible messenger" to impart the wisdom that Telemachus needed.

Figure 1.1. Mentoring in the age of the *Odyssey* and Athena

Source: Intueri/stock.adobe.com

While the poem *Odyssey* occurred during the Bronze Age, sometime in the 13th century BCE, we can imagine through Homer the different roles and different technologies available to Athena to bring home the understanding needed by young Telemachus.

In addition to these magical, mythical technologies, Mentor would have been limited to early oral communications to gather information and present it to young Telemachus concerning his father and the Trojan War. Perhaps they were able to receive communications from travelers familiar with the war or those who had received this information some time and somewhere before arriving back in Ithaca on their journeys.

Dispatches by ship would have provided the fastest route if they had arrived. These ancient ships could travel at speeds of up to six knots, which would have allowed them to make the 565 nautical mile journey and arrive in one to two weeks if they were able to proceed directly from one location to another. Resupply stops would have slowed the journey, perhaps lengthening it by another month. However, it took Odysseus more than ten years, to make the passage due to bad weather, resupply stops, and a series of delays outlined in *Odyssey*.

Theater and the arts would also have been available to Telemachus helping to ingrain information and support the oral histories relayed to him by Mentor.

THE TOOLS OF MENTORING

The tools of mentoring in those days would have been role models and oral tradition. Homer was only able to capture in writing the oral tradition of *Odyssey* near the end of the 8th Century BCE. Later Greek written documents would have included recorded histories, philosophy, and literature for future generations.

Homer was only able to capture in writing the oral tradition of *Odyssey* near the end of the 8th Century BCE.

As we spring forward in human history, we can mark the use of technologies through "social and industrial revolutions." We can look with some certainty at technologies that would have also improved mentoring during that age.

Although mentoring was still principally a face-to-face communication, one of the first technologies available for mentoring was papyrus, which enabled writing and recording information for future reference.

Oral traditions of history still provided the core of our information, while handwriting allowed us to pass on information more accurately over time. Basic handwriting on small sheets of parchment later became rolled-up scrolls for passing information and building libraries of knowledge. The technological advancement of writing on papyrus, parchment, or wax tablets, was made possible by the Greeks beginning in 1200 BCE. (Turner).

The printing press was the next major advance in communication, education, and mentoring, with the oldest known printed text originating in China during the first millennium AD.

> Basic handwriting on ... parchment [and]
> ... scrolls [allowed] passing information
> and building libraries of knowledge.

A Buddhist book, *The Diamond Sutra*, from Dunhuang, China during the Tang Dynasty in AD 868, is the oldest known printed book (History). It was created using block printing on panels of hand-carved wood blocks in reverse. Movable type using carved clay blocks arranged on an iron frame and pressed against an iron plate provided our next improvement in communication and printing. This innovation is attributed to Bi Sheng, from Yingshan, Hubei, China, who lived from approximately AD 972 to 1051. (Turner).

By 1127 to 1279 during the Southern Song Dynasty books and other printed material enabled the rise of the scholarly class and a status symbol for the wealthy (ibid).

However, it was the arrival of the printing press using metal printing blocks for each letter in 1440 by Johannes Gutenberg that provided one of the most significant technological improvements to expand the role of mentoring. Mentoring no longer relied solely on face-to-face communications or handwritten documents. Information could be quickly mass-produced and available to the many rather than just the select few.

> A Buddhist book, *The Diamond Sutra*, from ... the [Chinese] Tang Dynasty in AD 868, is the oldest known printed book. It was created using block printing ...

The rise of several Industrial Revolutions over the past 300 years has had an overwhelming impact on the advancement of industrial production and civilization itself. But it has not been just the industrial technological changes that have had an enormous effect on our society. It has been the information and communication technologies (ICT) that have been, and will continue to, make astronomical disruptive changes to our society.

MENTORING AND THE FIRST INDUSTRIAL REVOLUTION

The beginnings of the First Industrial Revolution can be traced to 1765 as mechanization began to replace the need for backbreaking labor in agriculture for sustenance living. The age of industry, as well as the mass extraction of coal and the invention of the steam engine, accelerated transportation, manufacturing, and our economies.

Information and communication technologies available in those days were also changing. Long before the days of telephones, computers, social media, and mass communications, people were communicating through handwritten letters, newspapers and, for the common people, limited supplies of books. Oral storytelling was still a mainstay of our information and communication, and news and information were seldom timely outside of the local neighborhood or village.

During the 1800s, this began to change as the nature of printing changed, allowing small pamphlets to be produced and distributed quickly among the citizens. These products were relatively inexpensive to produce and could be distributed quickly. Although newspapers were and remain popular forms of communication, small pamphlets could be produced more quickly and distributed to larger audiences than these daily or weekly newspaper communications (Howard).

In the United States, the Second Continental Congress recognized the importance of rapid communications and, in 1775 established the first American Postal Service. Subsequently, a federally funded and managed Postal Service was mandated by the American Constitution. Acting on this requirement, in 1789 the U.S. Congress passed an act creating the U.S. Post Office. From its humble beginnings of 75 post offices and only 1800 miles of routes the system began opening opportunities for greater communication and information exchange for the Americas, with one another, with Europe, and indeed the world (Marshall).

By the late 18th century, technological discoveries began leading to tremendous improvements in communications. This communication revolution was most visible in the United States and Great Britain beginning around 1760 as the speed of communications had rapidly begun to accelerate with the establishment of improved postal systems and more efficient newspaper printing and distribution (Albion). However, these improvements

Figure 1.2. Chappe's 18th Century "optical tachygraph" tower

Source: Erica Guilane-Nachez/stock.sdobe.com

were not limited to these countries. The speed of communications was also improving throughout the world.

In 1792, Claude Chappe, a French inventor, developed a practical semaphore* system known as the "Tachygraph" or "Fast Writer." The system sent a semaphore code from a series of high towers within line of sight many miles apart so that communications could be relayed from tower to tower. His system was eventually installed throughout France and was used until the 1850s when the electric telegraph systems replaced it (Tysoe).

Spanish scientist Francisco Salva Campillo created the forerunner of the telegraph in 1795. His system could send electrical

---

* Semaphores are systems that rely on vision to transmit line-of-sight messages. Such systems can use mechanically-configured "arms" like Chappe's towers had, flags, or lights. Examples still in use today are marine signaling flags and traffic lights. In fact, some languages, such as Spanish, refer to traffic lights as *semáforos* ("semaphores").

signals representing individual letters over a network of cables (Tysoe). By 1816, Englishman Francis Ronalds had created the first "long-distance" working electrical device by sending a series of pulses down a length of iron wire placed between wooden frames. These pulses represented individual letters over this network of cables and were able to sustain the signal for a distance of 13 km (8 miles) (ibid). American Samuel F. B. Morris patented the first telegraph in 1837, and by 1845 the first public telegraph line had opened in the United Kingdom. The world followed suit. Technologies had opened the flow of information for the First Industrial Revolution.

Mentoring during [the First Industrial Revolution] ... moved from **family education to apprenticeships** ... [and] became even more important ... as thousands of people [chased] the promise of good jobs.

Mentoring during this period moved from family education to apprenticeships associated with the rise of industry. More rapid transportation enabled migration from the countryside to the city. Information and communications technologies improved alongside other industrial advances. Mentoring became even more important during the Industrial Revolution as thousands of people left the countryside into the cities following the advance of industries and the promise of good jobs.

Role models and family mentors were left at home, while these adventurers came to the cities without the knowledge or experience about this bold new world. Mentees needed to select new mentors and develop new relationships to advance their careers. They chose peers and managers, as well as friends who had migrated into the cities ahead of them.

These new mentors used traditional oral communication in mentoring their protégés. The difference was that information was being disseminated far more freely through newspapers, pamphlets, and books to supplement their knowledge. Information could be acquired quickly through these media from around the world.

MENTORING IN THE SECOND INDUSTRIAL REVOLUTION

By 1875 to 1880 the beginning of the Second Industrial Revolution was taking place. Three major impacts defined this epoch (Stearns). International industrial developments outside the previously industrialized Western societies were on the rise. This was particularly evident in Russia, Germany, and Japan.

> [In 1876 Bell's] … telephone had arrived.… and quickly spread throughout the world … [and m]entors could now communicate long-distance …

The West itself was also retooling and changing its industrialization. As these Western economies expanded, so too did the search for resources throughout Africa, Asia, and Latin America, where food and mineral production to serve the expanding industrial areas was increasing (ibid). People throughout the world were moving from their local towns and villages seeking jobs and opportunity, and ultimately seeking mentoring to improve their position.

A real turn in communications technology occurred in 1876

when Alexander Graham Bell filed a patent for an "apparatus capable of transmitting speech." The birth of the telephone had arrived. Telephone and telegraph communications began to compete, and quickly spread throughout the world, ever-increasing the world's ability to communicate. Within ten years of its invention, the telephone had expanded through South America, Europe, Asia and into Africa (Tysoe).

Mentors could now communicate long-distance with their mentees. Those that had left home to venture to the city for work could now reach back to family mentors, as well as mentor younger siblings. Ideas could now be disseminated far faster than in the past, enabling new opportunities for mentoring.

THE MENTORING OF SRINIVASA RAMANUJAN

Consider Srinivasa Ramanujan, to whom this book is dedicated. His story is well known in India, and perhaps Great Britain, but lesser known in other parts of the world. He was born in 1887 in the village of Erode, some 400 kilometers (249 miles) southwest of Chennai, India. Although he did not speak until he was three years old, he completed his primary school in just two years and entered high school at the age of seven (Wavare). Ramanujan was a self-taught, self-motivated mathematical genius. We know little of his earliest mentors, but by 1903 he had matriculated from "Town High School with distinction and several prizes" (Rao).

According to Utpal Mukhopadhyay, however, it was the "support of his mentors and well-wishers" that catapulted him to success and fame within his short lifetime. A friend offered Ramanujan a book, *A Synopsis of Results in Pure and Applied Mathematics*, written by George Shoobridge Carr, which provided thousands of mathematical results from various branches of mathematics.

While no complete mathematical proofs were provided in the book, this gift ignited Ramanujan's genius, allowing him to prove the results of the problems in his own way (570-84). Fortunately,

Ramanujan had acquired the habit of recording his thoughts in mathematics in a series of notebooks.

Ramanujan attended the University of Madras in Chennai, India for his formal education. Despite his genius he was unsuccessful in passing examinations at the University of Madras in 1905 and 1906, marking the end of his formal education (ibid). He then spent five long years conducting his independent mathematical research.

Mentors must ... understand their limitations.... [and p]rotégés must ... be on the lookout for mentors and ... learn the art of perseverance.

By July 1909 Ramanujan could no longer support himself and began searching for a job. He was both fortunate and unfortunate during this time as he began meeting several prominent mathematicians such as V. Ramaswamy Iyer, who recognized his genius, but who "... had no mind to smother [Ramanujan's] genius by an appointment in the lowest rungs of the revenue department" (ibid).

Ramaswamy did, however, write a letter of recommendation for Ramanujan and sent him to see P. V. Seshu Iyer, Ramanujan's teacher at government College, Kumbhakonam, and now a professor at Presidency College, Madras (Mukhopadhyay). In turn, Sushu Iyer provided a note of introduction and sent Ramanujan to see Dewan Bahadur Ramachandra Rao, the Collector (a senior government administrator) of Nellore, for potential employment.

After several conversations, "Bahadur also thought that Ramanujan should not be bogged down by offering him a job..." (ibid). He did, however, recommend that Ramanujan should stay at Madras with Seshu Iyer, and that he, Bahadur, would contribute to Ramanujan's support during this time.

It was another year before Ramanujan was able to get a temporary job at the Office of Accountant General of Madras, but his job was terminated after only a few weeks. Shortly thereafter, he was sent to see S. Narayan Iyer, the Chief Accountant of Madras Port Trust, who became one of Ramanujan's mentors.

Through a series of interventions and recommendations, on 1 March 1912, Ramanujan "...was appointed as a Class III, Grade IV clerk in the Accounts Section of the Madras Port Trust." Through his work and mentorship with those at Madras Port Trust, he was soon to be "discovered" outside of India.

Ramanujan had been encouraged to read a research paper by the famous Cambridge mathematician Godfrey Harold Hardy. In doing so, he discovered a problem that had not yet been solved. He began researching the problem and soon discovered a formula which would solve the unknown quantity. Encouraged by Seshu Iyer, Ramanujan wrote a letter to Prof. Hardy explaining his solution.

Hardy replied to Ramanujan on 8 February 1913, stating that he was very much impressed by the theorems of Ramanujan. Sometime after, Hardy invited Ramanujan to go to England and work with him. Thus began a mentorship by Hardy of his protégé Ramanujan that would go on to shake the foundations of mathematics worldwide, and lead to Ramanujan's acceptance as a fellow in the Royal Society (Mukhopadhyay).

There are several lessons for both mentors and protégés in this vignette. The first concerns where mentors can be found. The answer: anywhere. All it takes is a concerned person with awareness, willing to develop a relationship and help someone else.

Mentors must also understand their limitations. In this scenario, there were several situations in which mentors realized limitations and that they were unable to mentor. They did however help their protégés find other mentors who could take them further.

Protégés must also be on the lookout for mentors and not be afraid to approach others for mentoring. In addition, protégés must learn the art of perseverance. It took many years of perseverance by Ramanujan to continue his work while demonstrating a willingness to be mentored. Ramanujan was constantly working to perfect his mathematical talents, while awaiting the right mentor to help him achieve success.

> Key enabling technologies … [like] computers, cellular phones, and the Internet … satellites, space communications, and exploration … provid[ed] an even faster pace of communication while accelerating the need for mentoring.

As we have seen, in the pre-digital era, mentorship primarily relied on face-to-face communication, handwritten correspondence, and oral traditions. The advent of the printing press in the 15th century allowed for the dissemination of written knowledge, enabling mentors to share their insights through printed materials. However, it was not until the 20th century that technology started playing a more direct role in mentoring with the introduction of telecommunication tools.

MENTORING IN THE THIRD INDUSTRIAL REVOLUTION

The dawning of the Third Industrial Revolution occurred in 1947. The telephone became a key technology for remote mentorship, enabling mentors and mentees to engage in conversations across distances. This marked a significant shift in mentoring dynamics, as individuals were no longer confined to geographical proximity for mentorship relationships. The rise of radio and television further expanded the reach of mentorship, allowing mentors to share their expertise with a broader audience.

With the advent of the internet and digital communication in the late 20th century, mentoring entered a new era. Email and online forums provided asynchronous communication channels, allowing mentors and mentees to connect at their convenience. And the World Wide Web facilitated the creation of virtual mentorship programs and platforms, breaking down geographical barriers and connecting individuals from different parts of the world.

Key enabling technologies in the Third Industrial Revolution included digital logic integrated circuits, computers, microprocessors, cellular phones, and the Internet. Each of these technologies in their way reduces the size of communication devices enabling radio and mobile devices such as cellular telephones to be available in the palm of your hand.

Technological advances also allowed mankind to develop satellites, space communications, and exploration. Humankind has gone from dreaming about the moon to walking on it. The digital revolution removed significant barriers to space exploration, and advanced research in all fields, including biotechnology, providing an even faster pace of communication while accelerating the need for mentoring.

Through digital technologies, global connections were shortened. It also gave rise to the theory of "Six Degrees of Separation," the concept that everyone on the planet is within six or fewer social connections away from one another.

Proposed in 1967 by Professor Stanley Milgram of Harvard University in his seminal work, *The Small World Problem*, Milgram conducted the now-famous postcard experiment challenging people to route postcards to a fixed recipient by passing them only through direct acquaintances (60-7). He discovered that the average number of intermediaries was between 4.4 and 5.7. Later research conducted in 2012 using approximately 721 million Facebook users resulted in an average separation of 3.74 intermediaries (Backstrom).

What does this mean for mentoring? The perfect mentor from anywhere on the planet may be only four intermediaries away.

ENTER THE FOURTH INDUSTRIAL REVOLUTION

The Fourth Industrial Revolution began at the dawn of the 21st century when the development of even more powerful technologies advanced industry and communications as well as how we create, store, and use information and information systems.

[World] leaders identified three key interconnected features relating to "… talent "[:] … the increased pace … in job destruction and job creation … [and] automation …
[; inadequate] education and training systems … [; and,] outdated cultural norms … [that] create roadblocks for gender parity.

The concept of the Fourth Industrial Revolution has been a topic of great concern for world leaders and business magnets and has been widely discussed at the World Economic Forum (Gleason). In a white paper developed by the World Economic Forum in 2017, leaders identified three key interconnected features relating to "how talent would be developed and deployed" in the Fourth Industrial Revolution (World). They identified the increased pace of change in job destruction and job creation along with the risk of automation. Automation, they surmised, would lead to one-third of all job skill sets becoming completely new within three years (World). In addition, the education and training systems of today are inadequate to meet these new job skills. Finally, the authors concluded that prevailing, outdated cultural norms and institutional inertia would create roadblocks for gender parity, with women having less than two-thirds of the economic opportunity of men.

The World Economic Forum Report identified several key action areas necessary to meet the demands of the Fourth Industrial Revolution. They identified education including professionalization of the teaching workforce as an additional 26 million teachers would be needed by 2030, as well as digital fluency, and early exposure to the workplace through ongoing career guidance. The report also highlighted how "technological and sociodemographic changes are shortening the shelf life of workers' skill sets" (ibid).

THE AGE OF ARTIFICIAL INTELLIGENCE

As a field of study, Artificial Intelligence, or AI, had its beginnings in 1956 at the Dartmouth Summer Research Project on Artificial Intelligence, with the goal to investigate how machines could be made to simulate various aspects of intelligence.

In reality, AI could be said to date back to the days of Aristotle in 322 BCE, for it was Aristotle who first formulated precise sets of laws governing the rational part of the mind. This logical framework allowed one to "generate conclusions mechanically, given initial premises" (Russell). Many other scientists from many different fields have over the years, contributed to the development of AI. One of the most influential was Alan Turing, who in the 1930s developed the idea of a formal model for computing machines created to simulate intelligence and how they might be tested (433-60).

In recent years, the integration of AI and ML (machine

learning) technologies has introduced new dimensions to mentoring. AI-powered platforms can analyze vast amounts of data to provide personalized recommendations and insights to mentees. Virtual reality (VR) and augmented reality (AR) technologies are also being explored to create immersive mentoring experiences, allowing individuals to engage in realistic simulated scenarios.

It is this exponential rise of technologies that has catapulted us into the Age of Artificial Intelligence where the use of AI in communications, education, and nearly every electronic device with which we interact has launched us into a new phase of mentoring—Mentoring Beyond AI.

[An] exponential rise of [AI, ML, VR, and AR] technologies ... has catapulted us into the Age of Artificial Intelligence ... [and] has launched us into a new phase of mentoring—Mentoring Beyond AI ... [that] must seamlessly incorporate both man and machine as never before.

In this new age of AI, mentoring must seamlessly incorporate both man and machine as never before. AI will be incorporated into every element of our society. Already, we rely on conversational AI technologies like Siri, Alexa, and Google Assistant to help us with our chores, provide entertainment and information, and be our companions. We are incorporating other advanced technologies, such as ChatGPT to help us in our communications through writing, presentations, and translations. Others are using these technologies to develop new art forms, create new businesses, and advance our virtual presence in the metaverse. Our educational and mentoring processes as well as our interpersonal relationships will, by necessity also be changed.

While mentoring has changed to meet the changing times, in its essence the mentoring core remains unchanged. In 2004, W. Brad Johnson and Charles R. Ridley analyzed thousands of books, journal articles, research reports, narrative accounts, and manuals for professionals in the art of mentoring. The result was a distillation of mentoring into fundamental skill sets, which they titled *The Elements of Mentoring*. These elements provide the fundamental "nuts and bolts of being a good mentor." But the mentoring experience is also an element of the technologies available to the mentor and protégé. Throughout this book we explore not only the fundamentals of mentoring but the technologies that assist us in doing so.

To fully understand the impact AI will have on mentoring in this new revolutionary age, it is important to understand what it means to be a mentor, a protégé or mentee, and the unique relationship that must be cultivated and nurtured on this journey.

■ ■ ■

KEY POINTS ABOUT MENTORING AND TECHNOLOGY

The roots of mentoring reach deep into our human prehistory where we as social beings strived to help others to be a productive part of our society. We attribute the term "mentor" to the Greek poet Homer, in his epic poem *Odyssey*, where the Greek king of Ithaca, Odysseus, upon leaving for the Trojan war, charges his good friend Mentor with the responsibility of seeing to his son Telemachus' education and life guidance while he is away.

As we move forward in human history, we tie the use of technologies through the ages to our ability to better mentor our protégés, moving from one-to-one oral traditions and living examples as a means of passing information to our protégés into our current Age of Artificial Intelligence.

Here we present the highlights of technological developments that have affected mentoring over the ages:

1. **Bronze Age.** From around 1300 BCE and earlier, teachings and ideas were conveyed by writing as glyphs on cave walls, stones, and orally from generation to generation, like the *Odyssey*, conceived as an oral poem around 1300 BCE.

1. **Classical period**. Homer captured the *Odyssey* in writing centuries after the Bronze Age, during the Classical period. This was the beginning of technology accelerating ever faster through the human experience providing a better means of mentoring through the ages.

2. **Early Chinese dynasties**. With the Chinese invention of the printing press during the first millennium AD, Buddhist monks were able to produce books in mass that captured the human experience, making it far easier to expand a storehouse of knowledge. Their technology used hand-carved wood blocks to create whole "pages" so that mentoring information could be rapidly produced, stored, and circulated for the use of the many rather than the elite few.

3. **Renaissance and Reformation periods**. The arrival of printing presses, invented by Johannes Gutenberg in the mid-15th Century, used metal printing blocks for each letter rather than the carved wood blocks of the early Chinese, and began the Renaissance and Reformation periods in Europe.

4. **First Industrial Revolution**. The advancement of mentoring from 1765 saw that mechanization began to replace the need for backbreaking labor, providing both opportunity and need for different types of mentoring, faster communi-

cation, and calls for more diverse degree options and new general education programs—a dramatic shift away from classical education (Penprase 978).

5. **Second Industrial Revolution.** This period came a hundred years later, with massive technological advancements in industries using new sources of energy, electricity, gas, and oil as well as development of better communications devices like the telegraph and telephone.

6. **Third Industrial Revolution**. By the 1970s the Third Industrial Revolution gave us the power of nuclear energy for societal benefit, as well as the revolution of electronics, telecommunications, and computers. This revolution removed the barriers to space exploration, advanced research, and biotechnology, providing an even faster pace of communication and an even greater need for mentoring.

7. **Fourth Industrial Revolution**. This started at the beginning of the 21st Century where even more powerful technologies have advanced industry and communications. It is this exponential rise of technologies that has catapulted us into the Age of Artificial Intelligence in communications, education, and personal assistance, and has launched us into a new phase of mentoring, still being defined and equipped.

This new "chapter" of our human experience in mentoring—blending the human mind with the lightning-quick, massive processes of machines—begins with the recent rapid adoption of AI and ... *it is just starting to be written now.*

2

Setting the Stage

The mark of the immature man is that he
wants to die nobly for a cause, while the mark
of the mature man is that he wants to live
humbly for one.

—Wilhelm Stekel

SUCCESSFUL PEOPLE HAVE first focused on themselves as they build their careers. The focus is almost entirely on the individual as they position themselves first in their education, and then continue to move through their career seeking advancement, position, power or prestige, and success.

Looking back, most if not all of us have had mentors at some point or at several key points in our career. Our mentors played a crucial role in facilitating and supporting us as we advanced. Mentoring is an essential means of providing guidance and support to people, especially young people as they embark on their careers or take on new leadership roles.

WHAT IS AND WHY BE A MENTOR?

The greatest benefit of being a mentor is to provide a pathway into the future for the next generation. Will Allen Dromgoole's classic poem titled, *The Bridge Builder,* sums up the goal of being a mentor.

The Bridge Builder

An old man going a lone highway
Came at the evening, cold and gray,
To a chasm and deep and wide,
Through which was flowing a sullen tide.

The old man crossed in the twilight dim;
The sullen stream had no fear for him;
But he turned, when safe on the other side,
And built a bridge to span the tide.

"Old man," said a fellow pilgrim, near,
"You are wasting strength with building here;
Your journey will end with the ending day;
You never again will pass this way;
You've crossed the chasm, deep and wide-
Why build you this bridge at the evening tide?"

The builder lifted his old gray head:
"Good friend, in the path I have come," he said,
"There followeth after me today,
A youth, whose feet must pass this way.

This chasm, that has been naught to me,
To that fair-haired youth may a pitfall be.
He, too, must cross in the twilight dim;
Good friend, I am building this bridge for him."

Another humanist and author, Douglas M. Lawson, once said, "We exist temporarily through what we take, but we live forever through what we give." It is in this light that we have developed this program to mentor the next generation of mentors and protégés to provide a cornerstone of learning and education. It is a process of giving back and a responsibility for us to focus on raising others to the next higher level.

We often think the role of a mentor is simple. Since some of us have been very successful in our lives and have learned many lessons, we think we can pass these lessons on easily to others. But such is not the case. Mentors also need training, guidance and support in developing effective mentoring programs, models or styles through which to pass on those lessons learned in life. Being a mentor is not easy. There are many nuances and programmatic details that can have a tremendous impact on outcomes for both the mentor and the mentee. Recent research in mentoring has indicated that "short-lived, less than positive mentoring relationships (a hallmark of programs that are not well designed) can actually have a negative impact on participating youth" (Garringer).

As is often said in the medical profession, "First, do no harm." It is our intention to make the mentoring program as successful for the mentee as possible, and also a rewarding experience for the mentor. It takes both mentor and mentee (or protégé) to be in the correct mindset to effectively gain the most from the relationship. To do so, we've established this as a guide to help each one of us achieve the most efficient and effective mentoring possible, and ultimately to raise our ourselves and others to our highest potential.

Before we move forward, we would like to clarify that in this book, we use the terms "mentee" and "protégé" interchangeably. We know that a "mentee" is one being "mentored," while a "protégé" is one who is "guided and protected" by another.

Older mentoring programs (and sometimes older mentors)

think the process is one where the mentee's mind is opened and the mentor simply pours in new knowledge. A protégé on the other hand was essentially in the shadow of an older, more experienced person or mentor, protected and positioned in business by the mentor.

In today's world, we consider mentoring more than just "pouring" knowledge into someone. Passing knowledge or skills alone is not mentoring. Mentoring is a relationship which allows both the mentor and mentee to learn from one another. It does not necessarily come from an older, wiser and positioned mentor. Mentoring can also be done by peers and near peers, older or younger. It is the relationship we stress, as learning and growth can flourish within that protected, non-competitive relationship where both mentor and protégé learn from one another, growing in maturity emotionally and cognitively.

A mentor is a friend, teacher, guide, parent, well-wisher, role model, counselor and a philosopher....

No other activity is likely to give a mentor as much joy as giving and sharing their lifetime of experiences with their peers, as well as the next generation. These opportunities will have a positive impact in many ways, not all of which will provide an immediate, visible change or reward. A mentor must be willing to "pay it forward," while knowing the impact of their actions will echo throughout future generations.

A final word about being a mentor is that through exemplary behavior we may have unintended, positive influences on mentees, or others, as Sidebar 6.1 on page 115 demonstrates.

PREPARING TO MENTOR

A mentor is a friend, teacher, guide, parent, well-wisher, role model, counselor and a philosopher, as K. V. Dishena points out in Sidebar 2.1 on page 31. Not everyone who excels in their respective fields can become mentors, as mentoring is something that arises naturally based upon personal characteristics and maturity. However, even those who are naturals can be trained further to enhance their skills.

Mentoring can be a very rewarding experience, yet there are many potential mentors who do not care to engage in the process. Why? One reason is that mentoring is very hard work, and if not done correctly can result in a bad experience for both the mentor and mentee. Our goal is to prepare the mentor in order to facilitate a smooth and rewarding mentoring experience. Preparing and working together to hone one's skills is indeed a challenge, but a most rewarding one if approached with an open learning mindset.

There are several reasons why mentoring is not at the top of everyone's list of goals. While most mentors have been exceptionally successful people, there are a variety of obstacles preventing these successful people from becoming effective mentors.

Truly successful people raise other people up with them. However, this takes intent, time and training. Many people do not have the confidence, experience, or the training to help others achieve equal or greater success. Many other successful people believe they received little assistance and found their own way in their business life and hence believe an independent approach is the best way to advance one's career. What came easily for them may be very difficult to communicate to others, especially those from the next different generations. So, the first element of mentoring is a desire to mentor, while the first obstacle that needs to be overcome is their feeling of insecurity in stepping into the role as a mentor and providing exceptional guidance.

Successful people may also have developed an ego along the way based upon their extraordinary success. However, mentors cannot be people who are self-centered. Mentors must be mentoring for the right reasons, that is they must place the mentee above themselves in order to spend time with them and raise them up to be more than either the mentor or the mentee could dream possible. The art and science of giving does not come easily to everyone. The satisfaction derived through the success of one's mentee has to be experienced.

> Truly successful people raise other people up with them. However, this takes intent, time and training ... [and] mentors cannot be ... self-centered.

Each person is also different from every other person. While we may have many characteristics in common with successful people, we may not be able to explain why one person is successful and another is not. Self-help books tend to distill those key characteristics of the rich and famous that we can develop to assist us in our own success. However, it is our differences, especially differences in learning that must be discerned and cultivated to pass on success. Every person has characteristics that if properly cultivated can lead to success. But these characteristics must be discovered. The mentor must have the capacity to find these characteristics in others and help the mentee cultivate the seeds. To do this requires the mentor to have a commitment to the mentee with a genuine desire to focus on the other individual. A mentor must consider a person's gifts, temperament, passions, previous successes, happiness, and opportunities in order to discern the characteristics of growth.

Most importantly, the mentor must be able to determine their mentee's learning strengths and capitalize upon it.

Recognizing Purpose in Life

In order to be successful in life, one must recognize those threads that tie them to their purpose and ignite their passion and genuine interest in life to reach their maximum potential. Unfortunately, the average person often finds it difficult to recognize their passion, interest and abilities and work towards fulfillment which defines their purpose in life.

People often assume as they continue life's journey that at some point in time they will magically discover their purpose. More often, it is only on looking back at our lives that we can see the threads that defined our successful pathway. Sadly, some of us may never reach this point of discovery. A successful mentor can help others find their purpose in life, or at least set them on a path of discovery from which they will meet success. To be able to discern these things for others requires a commitment and a willingness to invest in others.

Mentoring Training and Skills

Many mentors have been unsuccessful in developing their mentees due to a lack of training. Mentoring is not a skill that most people learn in school or on the job, even if you are a successful coach, teacher or professor. Successful educators have likely been trained to disseminate information and evaluate a group of students rather than walk alongside a single person as a friend, philosopher and guide to be able to bring that individual to their highest level. Skills in the classroom or the boardroom may not equate to successful mentoring relationships.

Facilitating individuals to advance in their career requires more than a capacity to communicate information or train in particular skills. We see this daily as we develop multiple training programs in the business community that are not successful in moving all employees continuously up the ladder of success. Teaching and learning are complex processes involving a vast array of variables, not the least of which are a desire to learn, the opportunity to learn and grow, and an inherent knowledge that there are no "glass ceilings" holding them back.

Mentors must understand their own self-worth, and cultivate self-esteem in others. If a mentee doesn't feel good about himself or herself, the mentee will never not be able to believe they can be a success, regardless of how much they accomplish. But a person who has confidence in their potential, is primed to move to higher levels. Encouragement is a key factor enabling mentees to develop their own self-worth. While constructive criticism is needed in advancing the growth of an individual, the mentor must temper criticism with a spirit of approval and encouragement.

Research suggests that people with a bad experience which has dampened their enthusiasm can overcome this experience, as people are naturally motivated to succeed. Every young child has a natural curiosity that must be cultivated in all areas of their life. Far too many people have been beaten down by lack of support, adopted bad attitudes from those around them, or have experienced lack of appreciation by supervisors, teachers, parents, coaches or peers which have left them motivationally destitute. Mentors must understand this and help their mentees to overcome bad experiences and re-energize them to reach their full potential.

The Mentoring Relationship

Mentors must also realize their limitations, some of which occur through no fault of their own. In particular, mentors must understand that people must "buy in" to their mentor before they are able to open themselves up to be mentored.

Mentoring is also a two-way street and an opportunity for both,

Sidebar 2.1. A mentor recognizes a diamond in the rough

JOEL RODRIGUEZ, SCIENCE DEPARTMENT CHAIR & TEACHER
Center for International Education, A Cambridge Associate School, Homestead, Florida

Fresh out of college and inexperienced in my new job as a teacher made for a very difficult time adapting to my new career. Consequently, the school's administration was contemplating letting me go, except for one former teacher. He had many successful years of experience in the classroom, which included winning teacher-of-the-year on multiple occasions, giving his opinion greater influence in these decisions.

During this trying time for me he had left the classroom and was on his way to becoming a school administrator—and he intervened on my behalf. This alone is enough to be grateful but he went even further and took me under his wing, becoming one of the most important mentors I've had the pleasure to learn from. In retrospect I believe that there were two aspects of our mentor-mentee relationship that made it not only functional, but an opportunity for both of us to grow.

The first of these was the fact that he was always available to give suggestions and pass down any wisdom he had on any matter. I use the word "suggestions" purposely because he never directed me to do anything in any fashion. He would make suggestions that I could then either use or not, at my discretion, and many times his suggestions would influence my decisions, shaping them into a form that I otherwise would not have conceived on my own.

Secondly, our relationship involved a lot of self-reflection from both parties. This came in the form of me discussing any issues that I had been having and reflecting on whether my actions were successful or not. In turn, my mentor would then comment on my ideas and with his suggestions he would discuss his experiences with similar situations. This involved the same level of self-reflection on whether or not he thought the actions he took were successful, which led to the explanation of why he was making his suggestions.

This self-reflection was probably one of the biggest influences in my opinion of him as a mentor, not only because it gives us new insight into different ways to approach a problem; it also made it so that we were both learning and growing from our relationship. And it leaves me yearning for the opportunity to pass on this wisdom and help someone grow into a better individual as my mentor did me.

mentor and mentee, to learn from each other, as Sidebar 2.1 illustrates. However wise or experienced a mentor may be, there is always something more to learn, and oftentimes it is the mentee who surfaces a fresh idea for both to explore. As children can renew in observing parents the forgotten joys of life, so can mentees give a new perspective or a renewed vision to a problem that the experienced mentor may have put behind or forgotten about.

Trust, mutual respect, and agreement are key to the mentoring process. Many of us have experienced leading through "position" where we have been appointed or earned positions to lead others. However, people will not always follow good people in authority. Successful mentoring is similar to successful leadership, which occurs when people follow you another because they believe in you. Only then will a mentee be open to a mentor's suggestions.

Being a mentor demands that you strive to deeply understand people. The mentor must have highly developed people skills and genuine concern for others. The more natural this process is to the mentor, the more successful the mentor will be.

PROGRAM QUALIFICATIONS FOR MENTORS

Many formal mentoring programs have age qualifications of 50 years or older in order to qualify as a mentor. The thinking is that with age comes the maturity to form successful mentor-mentee relationships. We believe that mentoring takes place at all ages and stages of life and the only age qualification for mentors is to be old enough to understand they still have a lot to learn themselves, but young enough to be enthusiastic about passing on lessons about skills, knowledge, information and experiences they have learned in life. We look for mentors who have distinguished themselves through success in their chosen fields of endeavor, and as well as those who can communicate their successes to the needs and experiences of others. It is, after all, a relationship.

The most important qualification a mentor can have is a desire to work with and be accessible to their mentee. This requires a commitment on behalf of the mentor and the mentee to establish and maintain a working relationship with each other.

A mentor's characteristics should include positiveness,

Sidebar 2.2. The importance of a mentor's own example

BALDEV RAJ, DIRECTOR
National Institute of Advanced Studies, Bengaluru, India

My mother, although she was not highly educated, was my first and truest mentor among many. She helped me fulfil my expectations and aspirations. As a child, I followed her faithfully, obediently, patiently. Her logical and simple ways were encouraging, and she allowed me to make my own decisions. As I grew up and slowly faced life I discovered the qualities of hard work and ethical behavior she instilled in me. What I learned through her examples has been the foundation of everything I've accomplished in life.

At this point, I should mention that my father died when I was 11 years old. That, despite the very limited finances and possibilities at her command, made her the provider and guide for our large family of five brothers and one sister. She molded me and my siblings under very challenging circumstances with important qualities and life lessons:

Compassion. She could forgive her most severe opponents within and outside the family. She selflessly gave financial, material, and emotional support to those who did not have resources. To help me develop compassion she would give me pocket money and would give me the option to spend it on myself or for helping someone needy with meals, clothes, education, or something else. I learned compassion and charity, without an ego, from her. She considered this to be a good human being.

Ethics. Despite the difficulties she faced, she did not look for resources from others or take advantage of anyone.

Self-learning. Our family's business was very small she had no one in the family or within our network to guide her. Her example, working hard while balancing our challenges and quality of life, encouraged me to work hard and stay focused.

My rewards were simple but heart-felt and effective: almond milk, hugs, affection, and her captivating smiles. She motivated me to learn through trial and error.

warmth, openness, and patience, as well as an intense willingness to listen twice as much as speaking. Additionally, Baldev Raj adds compassion, ethics, and self-learning as desirable characteristics for a mentor (Sidebar 2.2).

Our program emphasizes the old adage that "our Creator endowed us with two ears with which to hear, but only one mouth with which to speak." The mentor must realize the principal goal of mentoring is to use the mentor's education and experience to enlighten and guide the mentee. This requires a keen ability to understand the mentee's experience, stage in life, capacity to learn, and motivation level in order to impart knowledge.

In addition, mentors need to set limits for the mentee and, if in a formal program, respond to both the Program Administration Supervisor, and the Supervisor of the mentee. A formal program will provide new and interesting methods to impart knowledge, so mentors may often find themselves in a student role in which they can better connect and share their experiences.

Formal programs may also require mentors to travel to activity sites, or use modern technology to connect with mentees. This may require a great deal of patience in dealing with program idiosyncrasies.

RESPONSIBILITIES OF A MENTOR

Mentors must be available and willing to play and serve in a variety of roles within the mentoring program. Mentors first and foremost, will serve as friends to their mentees and to one another. Mentors must be able to advocate effectively and fluently to their students, as well as to other mentees and program administrators.

In their role as mentors, individuals will take on the responsibility of being a guide, as well as a listener to the mentee on all aspects of their life, including their personal life, activities in school or work, potential career advisors, and other areas as the mentee is willing to share.

Most effective mentoring requires meeting with the mentee either face-to-face, through telecommunication, or other modern communication method for a minimum of two hours every week. This is essential in order to build and maintain the necessary rapport that is a "must" between the mentor and mentee. These sessions can be used by the mentor to set and evaluate goals for the mentee, as well as share in their personal lives.

In formal mentoring programs, mentors will also be required

Sidebar 2.3. A trial by fire forges a real mentor

EDDA RIVERA, CHAIRPERSON & TEACHER
John A. Ferguson Senior High School, Miami, Florida

In August 1995 I became a teacher after other careers in computer programming and business. At new teachers' orientation I and others were told about all the support that we were going to receive. I was excited! Having raised three children of my own I knew how to manage children's behaviors, and I considered myself well-versed in the sciences. I went confidently into my new role.

My first teaching assignment was a temporary position in a rough-and-tumble inner-city middle school. What an experience! I was assigned to a math class for special education students, but my preparation was to teach science. Although I asked repeatedly for guidance and supplies, they never materialized. I found myself trying to survive in a hostile environment.

Later in the same year I was offered a permanent position in a high school, still in the inner-city. I was glad for two reasons: I got a permanent teacher spot, and I was going to teach science, my passion. As I got to my new job, I was introduced to the special education department chairperson who was supposed to be my mentor, and having a department chair as my mentor made me feel sheltered.

Starting late that year as a permanent teacher for special education students who had scared out substitute teachers all that year was a tough mission. To boot, my classroom was in the farthest, most deplorable, portable classroom there was. I was scared: of the condition of the portable, of the students' attitudes and behaviors, about the school gangs and fights, but mostly scared of not being able to grow into the professional I envisioned myself to be because I felt so lost. And my "mentor" only responded to my pleas for help with "I'll be there soon" and soon never happened.

One day, tired of waiting for help and support, I decided to take control. Control of the classroom, control of the students' attitudes and behaviors, and control of my career. I gained my students' attention and respect with my resume as an experienced computer programmer and a business manager, and my personal background. Next, I befriended the school's security for support controlling students' behaviors, and the personnel in the main office to get things done. When my requests to my chairperson for books and teaching materials went unheeded I went over her head and directly to the principal—this time not asking but demanding—and reminding the principal that I was hired to teach and not to babysit students.

When I asked my department chair (I no longer considered her my mentor) for science materials she laughed and referred me to the science department. And that's when the battle started: I was sent back and forth between the special

A trial by fire forges a real mentor (Continued)

education and science departments until, fed up, I went back to the principal and requested a meeting with both department chairs and himself. The meeting was granted and everything changed gradually from there on.

After a couple of years of battle that felt like an eternity I had gained the respect and support from the school administration and from the science department's chairperson. I transferred into the science department and eventually became its chairperson. And I realized that I learned so much from the abandonment that I had to give back to others who followed.

There is not a day in my life now that I don't mentor someone, whether it's a fellow coworker, a student, a friend or someone I just

met. The feeling of being lost and not having a person for direction or for support is terrifying for some. It was for me. I am not the kind of intrusive person that gets into everybody's business. I am mostly a passive listener who is always willing to help when help is needed or asked for; one who is always there for support, or an ear, or a word of advice.

Now, as the science department's chairperson, I make sure all the teachers, especially those new to the system, have everything they need to succeed. As a teacher, I make sure I provide my students with all the tools they need to excel in school and in the future.

People will be more receptive and willing to better themselves when they feel supported and guided than when they feel lost.

to participate in training programs and supervisory meetings with the program's administrative staff. These programs will be established and implemented in order to provide maximum training for the mentor within the time constraints of their active lives. In addition, mentors will be required to participate in some special group events and activities throughout the year. Due to the nature of various programs, especially international mentoring, events should be held to a minimum and agreed-upon before the mentor takes up their responsibilities.

Mentors may also be required to evaluate the program, their mentees, as well as themselves and their effectiveness in the program. This will require a 365° look at mentor as well as mentee behaviors. Honest assessments are essential to ongoing improvements in the mentoring programs.

However, not everyone is suited for mentoring, nor is everyone willing to assume the role. When mentors fail in their responsibilities an entire program—or even an entire institution—can be put at risk because it can result in demoralized talent. Gifted mentees are the future of their institution or industry, and they need effective guidance and nurturing to realize their potential. Sidebar 2.1 on page 31 demonstrates a positive example of a caring mentor who saved a struggling novice teacher; and Sidebar 2.3 on page 35 presents a negative example of how unprepared or unwilling mentors can hurt their own cause.

In the latter case, Ms. Rivera, already an experienced business-woman, survived as a teaching "mentee" only through her resourcefulness, and her willingness to confront the problems that were hampering her development as a special education teacher. A less experienced person would have simply quit. But Ms. Rivera turned her negative experience as a mentee to learn and put to practice lessons about what positive and effective mentoring should be.

PREPARING TO MENTOR

Mentors must be prepared to assume a variety of roles and relationships with their mentees. Many of these roles will overlap and change as the relationship of the mentor - mentee grows over time. As in all successful relationships, the number of roles the mentor will take on will increase significantly as the relationship deepens and develops over time. Some of the most important roles mentors must play are described in the following paragraphs.

Teacher–Trainer

In this role, the mentor assumes the role of teacher or trainer, imparting knowledge and technical expertise to the mentee. Mentors will use their experience as a guide to provide learning opportunities for the mentee. This is an extremely powerful role, especially for former teachers and university professors, as well as professionals in engineering arts and sciences who can impart their specific past experiences on to the next generation of students. When people think of mentoring, this is the most common role in which they see a mentor—mentee relationship.

Resource Supporter–Advocate

Closely related to the Teacher-Trainer role is the Resource Supporter-Advocate. In this role, the mentor works, speaks and acts on behalf of the mentee in helping the mentee access community and business resources. This is a critical role in supporting entrepreneurship and business startups.

Positive Role Model

In all roles, the mentor must perform as a positive role model for the mentee. This is not to hide past failures or cover over mentor weaknesses, but to demonstrate values that the mentor wishes to be ingrained within the mentee. The mentor's verbal identification of his own weaknesses and past failures is actually a strength, as he is modeling for the mentee how to realistically assess oneself and learn and grow from this experience. This will help the mentee understand life's ups-and-downs, and how to navigate them as effectively as possible.

Nevertheless, in all other activities the mentor must strive to provide the positive role model for their mentees by upholding those standards of excellence and integrity and responsibility demanded of world-class leaders today.

Mentors must … assume a variety of roles
and relationships with their mentees.

Social Supporter and Guide

In this role mentors provide encouragement to the mentees as they embark on new experiences. This is a critical role in the transition from secondary schools into the colleges and universities, especially if the colleges and universities are far from the traditional support base of the mentee. During these transition phases, mentees will experience many new and important opportunities, and must be encouraged to harness these opportunities for their own development. In other words, these opportunities provide the individuals the space to spread their wings and experience new opportunities. However, it's also important for the mentor to guide the mentee during these times to avoid potential pitfalls. When mentees lose their traditional support base, traditional values may also be abandoned. In many cases, students will be studying with other students representing different cultures and values. This can be a time of experimentation, in which the mentees will need additional support, guidance and encouragement.

Friend and Companion

Another important role for the mentor is that of a friend and companion to the mentee. It is important that the mentor be consistently available, and in all cases sincere in the advice, counsel and friendship towards the mentee. The best relationship with the mentee is that of a caring friend, whose friendship is in all cases unconditional.

Challenger

At times the relationship of the mentor will need to be that of a challenger or coach. In this role the mentor must provide honest assessment coupled with a firm encouragement to the mentee to maximize the mentees potential and future success. In many cases it is also important to take a back seat and challenge the mentees to think for themselves and to provide their own opinions. A well-disciplined mentor will also be able to provide firm guidance and draw out the mentee to become an independent leader, a logical thinker who distinguishes facts from opinions that are part of our worldview.

The goal of all mentoring is to provide support to vulnerable mentees through the development of a meaningful relationship with a mature, successful mentor. Over time the relationships will change based upon the needs of the mentee, but in all cases this relationship should grow in a bond of deep trust between the mentor and mentee.

It is important that essential guidelines be incorporated into the mentor's values. These guidelines include:

1. **Reliability**. Mentors should maintain their relationship with their mentees by meeting the mentee at the specific time described. If there is a problem it is essential that the mentor call to cancel the appointment. Nothing can damage the mentor—mentee relationship more than a series of broken appointments, as this decreases the mentees trust in the relationship and in the individual.

2. **Consistency**. Short, regular contacts will accomplish more in the long run than a series of irregular meetings. Consistency in the approach taken during these meetings is also essential in building trust by the mentee. Both the mentors and the mentees must know what the expectations are for the meetings. While deviations may be both necessary and desirable under certain circumstances, the basic mentoring message must be consistent throughout the relationship.

3. **Focus**. It is absolutely essential that the mentor focus on and develop a primary relationship with the mentee. This should be in the form of uninterrupted one-on-one meetings with the mentee. The mentee should feel as if he or she is the most important person in life to that mentor when they are together and building their relationship. Avoid including the mentee's family members except on rare occasions, as this is a diversion from the development and bonding of a one-on-one relationship with the mentee.

4. **Respect**. Respect is essential in the mentoring relationship in many ways. First and foremost is respect for the individual mentee, which should be reciprocated to the mentor. Secondly, it is essential that the mentor respect the mentee's family and the parents' wishes for their children. The mentor's role is not to replace the parents, but rather to provide an outside source of inspiration and experience for the mentee. The mentor should provide periodic reports to the mentee's parents about the mentee's progress. In addition, remember that mentors are not to share personal information with outsiders about the mentee and/or the mentee's family. If these areas are respected, the mentor will be able to develop a strong relationship with both the mentee and the mentee's family.

5. **Question.** Mentorship and mentorship programs are team efforts and everyone is a part of the team. Your success may be the key to unlocking another mentor's success with their student. If you are having problems, ask other mentors for assistance. Remember that the only way to really understand your mentee is to ask about their lives, dreams and aspirations.

6. **Praise**. Another essential element of the mentoring equation is for the mentor to provide positive feedback to the

mentee. When life seems most difficult a pat on the back or a word of encouragement can make the difference between success and failure, or be the difference between failure as a learning point or a finishing point. Encourage them to succeed!

7. **Safety First!** At all times be keenly aware of your surroundings and the dangers that may exist within your mentees environment. Be prepared to intervene.

8. **Fiscal Responsibility**. A part of your mentoring responsibilities includes fiscal responsibilities for both yourself and your mentee. In addition to teaching your mentee fiscal responsibility, it is essential that you demonstrate the same. Be careful in additional activities that you may be conducting with your mentee that you do not over extend your financial resources, or spend money too freely, as the mentee may develop unrealistic expectations which could damage your relationship.

9. **Imagination**. Use your imagination and creativity on ways to work with your mentee and to develop close bonds and relationships. Don't be afraid to try new things which can be fun and educational. Encourage your mentee to be imaginative. Harness their creativity and innovative ability.

10. **Culture**. Regardless of who you are and where you are mentees and their family members may embrace different traditions, values and cultures than you. Be open-minded, understanding, and respectful of cultural differences.

11. **Limits and Expectations**. Respect for one another also means that proper limits of conduct must be established and maintained. Harsh or tyrannical treatment will not be

condoned. Nor will unreasonable demands by mentees be accepted. Politely discuss the limitations and the basis of your differences when they occur. If differences cannot be worked out, the issue must be raised to the program administrators.

12. **Inclusion.** Mentees should participate with their mentors in decision-making concerning joint activities. Mentors should also encourage creativity and development of strategic planning skills by the mentee.

13. **Timeliness**. Mentors should complete all forms and information required by the program in a timely manner.

14. **Humor**. A sense of humor is imperative to success of the program. Keep your sense of humor intact. Contact the administrative staff when difficulties arise, and keep your mentee informed of all relevant information. Most importantly, relax, be yourself, and enjoy the program to the fullest! There is no greater achievement than developing and maintaining a successful mentor—mentee relationship.

CONFIDENTIALITY OF RELATIONSHIPS AND PROGRAMS

In your role as a mentor or program administrator, you will occasionally have access to private and personal information about your mentee and their family. This information is privileged information, and must be kept private with no unauthorized discussion outside of the formal program.

During mentoring and instructional sessions with other mentors, you will be encouraged to share information about your relationship. Share only essential information necessary to help you improve the situation, or that you judge will not harm the mentee or other family members in any way.

If you are in a formal program, you may be asked to sign a

statement attesting your understanding of the programs policies on confidentiality. It is therefore important for you to understand situations in which it may be necessary to share information that you consider confidential.

There may be some circumstances in which it is necessary to share information with appropriate staff members or others concerning the mentoring program. If in a formal program, do not attempt to contact public officials on your own concerning your mentee or their family. Always contact a staff member who may assist you in handling issues of youth safety. The administrative staff point of contact should be your first point of contact if you expect any of the following:

1. Your mentee is in danger of hurting himself or herself.

2. Your mentee is in danger of being hurt by someone else.

3. Your mentee is in danger of hurting someone else.

A part of your training program will include confidentiality policies, and the proper procedures to follow should any of the above situations arise. Do not hesitate to follow up with the program staff to gain further clarity and insight in any of these issues.

After you are matched with your mentee it is important that you develop a regular meeting schedule. As your relationship grows, your mentee's expectations will also grow. Do not disappoint them by arbitrarily canceling meetings. Certain situations cannot be avoided such as illnesses, important business trips or vacations, or unexpected problems.

To avoid cancellations, even in these unexpected situations, plan ahead. Let your mentee know as far in advance as possible of your unavailability, and remind each other of alternative dates. If a meeting is canceled, rescheduled the meeting with the mentee as soon as possible. Make sure you advise the mentee of why you are unable to meet, and let the mentee know as soon as possible that you will contact them concerning the follow up meeting. Also, inform the staff of your planned absences and intended date of return.

Should you encounter a medical emergency ... **call emergency medical personnel**, and the parent or guardian....[I]n a formal mentoring environment and ... [it is] a *nonlife-threatening* situation ... call the program coordinator!

For unexpected problems, contact both the mentee and the program coordinator as soon as possible to inform them of the situation.

EMERGENCY ACTIONS

Should you encounter a medical emergency at any time ... call emergency medical personnel, and the parent or guardian.

If you are in a formal mentoring environment and encounter a *nonlife-threatening* situation that could be a *potential emergency* concerning the mentee ... call the program coordinator!

The program coordinator may have additional information to assist you in whatever crisis the mentee may be encountering. The program coordinator can also assist you in contacting the parents or guardians and work with you and the mentee to resolve the situation.

Here is a final rule if the emergency relates to your mentee and the program coordinator is NOT immediately available:

Call the parent or guardian, as well as emergency medical personnel if appropriate.

For any emergency that should arise, be sure to *take appropriate life-saving measures first* and, at an appropriate time complete a program Incident Report.

GRIEVANCE PROCEDURES

Program Coordinators should handle grievances in the most expeditious manner. If you have a grievance or complaint, please first talk to the Program Coordinator. After sharing your concerns with the coordinator, if you are still not satisfied, make an appointment to talk to a member of the Senior Mentoring Advisory Group (SMAG), who will be able to resolve the situation or direct you to the next steps.

SAFETY TIPS

It is essential that mentors assess the risks of all activities involved in this program, and terminate any activities in which the mentor or mentee is not completely comfortable. In dangerous situations, it's important to learn what to do to avoid and or minimize problems. Use the "Three A's"—awareness, alertness, and avoidance—as helpful hints to make sure you are safe in any environment. As common-sensical as they are, we list them here because we can forget or ignore them at times:

Awareness
- Be aware of your surroundings.
- Plan ahead.
- Be prepared.
- Know your route. Use well-lighted and well-travelled roads.
- Let someone know the route you will take and when you plan to arrive.

- Walk with a purpose. Don't walk aimlessly toward your car or public transportation.
- Avoid wearing conspicuous jewelry.
- Do not carry large sums of money or credit cards.
- Keep a hand firmly on your purse/briefcase as you walk. If someone tries to grab your items, especially if the assailant is armed, let it go!
- Have keys ready if you are walking to your car or house. Don't fumble in your purse or pocket for them.

Alertness
- Be alert to potential dangers.
- Be alert to any activity near you.
- Be suspicious of people approaching your car asking for directions or change, or giving out flyers.
- Always give your car a quick inspection for any tampering.
- Check door handles, locks, and back seat before entering. If you think someone has tampered with your car, don't enter it.
- If you must travel with valuables, always keep them out of view.

Avoidance
- Avoid situations in which the mentor or mentee could be harmed such as meetings and activities in where you or the mentee may have to pass secluded, poorly lighted areas, especially at night.
- Avoid meeting where others may be able to overhear the conversation.
- Also, avoid meeting where the mentees' peers may encounter the mentee with you, as this could lead to embarrassment or bullying. The mentee will let you know when they have established a relationship with you in which they are comfortable meeting you and introducing you to their peers.

■ ■ ■

KEY POINTS ABOUT SETTING UP

Mentors have played a crucial role in facilitating and supporting others in their education and professional careers. Mentoring is an essential means of providing guidance and support to people, especially young people as they embark on their careers or take on new leadership roles.

But why be a mentor? Mentors provide a pathway into the future for the next generation. As Will Allen Dromgoole's classic poem, *The Bridge Builder*, finalizes,

> *This chasm, that has been naught to me,*
> *To that fair-haired youth may a pitfall be.*
> *He, too, must cross in the twilight dim;*
> *Good friend, I am building this bridge for him."*

Mentoring is about providing a pathway for the current and next generation. It can take on many aspects. A mentor passes valuable knowledge, skills, experiences, and education to another through a very important, cultivated relationship.

Not every successful person can become a mentor, as mentoring is something that arises naturally based on personal characteristics, maturity, and a relationship built with the mentee or protégé. The "mentee," or "protégé," on the other hand is a person who is willing to form a relationship with another to benefit from the experience. Trust, mutual respect, and an agreement to a mentoring pathway are key to the mentoring process.

Here are some key points to being a mentor:

1. In this book we use the term mentee or protégé interchangeably. Although we usually consider mentees and protégés to be younger than the mentor, this is not always the case.

2. Mentors must be prepared for their responsibilities and be able to understand and move between various roles. These roles include the Teacher—Trainer, Resource Supporter — Advocate, Positive Role Model, Social Supporter and Guide, Friend and Companion, and Challenger.

3. The most important aspect of all these roles for the mentor is CONFIDENTIALITY in the relationship. Mentors must always incorporate special guidelines within their values. These guidelines include reliability, consistency, focus, respect, a questioning attitude, a complementing and praising attitude, creativity, cultural understanding, and most importantly a sense of humor.

4. Finally, mentors must also know when to call others for assistance and how to respond when encountering emergencies with their protégés.

P A R T

II

The Mentoring Process

This section discusses what is required in the mentoring process to understand the multiple elements involved, including:

- how we learn,

- how mentors can build relationships with protégés,

- the mentoring mindset mentors need to meet the challenges,

- understand the behaviors of mentees, and

- understand and analyze communications with protégés from a multicultural, gender, and racial perspective.

CHAPTER

3

Learning, Mentoring, and Youth

Education is not the filling of a pail,
but the lighting of a fire.

—William Butler Yeats

EARLY MENTORING IS a key component to childhood development and complements education, life skills training and coaching. Supportive relationships formed between mentors and protégés provide both immediate and long-term benefits to our youth. Research indicates that early mentoring leads to better academic performance, better school attendance and all-around positive attitudes in life (Youth; Guryan 877).

Mentorship runs the full gamut of the educational experience from pre-K through college (and even into our professional lives) and can be viewed as a "holistic support system" for many students who may not have received adequate academic and social support earlier in their education (Graham 2). Studies have confirmed that student absences are indicative of poor academic performance and lower GPAs. New data suggests that mentoring can significantly reduce absences for all students, but particularly for students of color, and increase retention rates for high school and college students.

Who should be a mentor? Anyone with the characteristics, values, and inclinations to do so. However, recent research has confirmed the results of earlier studies indicating female students are more likely to pick female mentors and male students more likely to pick male mentors. Additionally, students of different cultural and racial backgrounds tend to respond better when mentors are similar to themselves (Erkut 415-6).

Role models in all areas of life are essential to our development. When a mentor who is a positive role model also becomes knowledgeable about his protégé's academic, personal, and professional environments, he can maximally contribute to his protégé's holistic development. A mentor who supports a student's academic career has proven to be especially important for minority, underrepresented students, and students of color in educational as well as professional settings (Stromei 58; Ishiyama 12).

A successful role model-mentor understands the role learning plays in each stage of their protégés' lives, then develops successful strategies for their mentees that are age and life appropriate.

CHILDHOOD AND LEARNING

The youth of today are in most respects, the same as today's mentors. Mentors may have forgotten their early adolescence and the physical, intellectual, social and emotional changes that were ongoing at that time. It's important that they re-familiarize themselves with these elements before they can properly assume a mentoring mindset for today's youth.

Before we look at the various stages of an individual's

Sidebar 3.1. The many mentors in our lives

K. V. DINESHA, PROFESSOR (RETIRED)
Indian Institute of Information Technology, Bangalore, India

About 30 years back, I took a course on screenplay writing for films. The teacher related to us the following pattern in the structures of mythological stories and classical movie scripts. He said:

"Initially the hero is just an observer of events around him until some event forcibly drags him to participate in the other events. A mentor/guide who knows about the dynamics of the events guides the hero. This goes on until he alone needs to fight to get out of that situation. He wins when he comes out successfully. Subsequently he becomes a mentor to another person."

This pattern explains a few aspects of mentor-mentee relationships.

Everyone will have mentors in each stage of their life. Our parents are the first mentors in our early days. Subsequently, elders in the family may play the role of mentors in various ways. Our primary, high school and college teachers are the mentors at the next level. These people are a strong influence in building our value system, attitude, and habits.

Parents as mentors are primarily responsible. They impose their value system and help us to build our own. Most of the time they switch between being rewarding, punishing, kind, and harsh, or a mix of these.

When I was in primary and high school, my parents wanted me to go to a Hindu mission every Sunday morning. There we enjoyed many activities, including sports and music. Many times instead of the religious "Sunday classes" I would watch a cricket match at the mission. When I returned home, I would announce, "I am returning from Sunday classes." My father knew it was only half true, but he didn't question me further. Perhaps he weighed the gain of my just going to the mission, even if I didn't always attend the Sunday classes. When I think back now, I feel he was right in his judgement—the give-and-take he probably considered. He guided me but he let me navigate through my own development.

The next phase in an individual's life may be college, or on to a workplace. Here we seek mentors actively to achieve a purpose, or to identify a purpose in our lives. In my case, I attended college, and after many years I earned a PhD in physics. All my mentors were passionate about their work, kind and understanding towards students, and at the same time *made clear their expectations.*

development throughout life, beginning with the early years, we should remember that we invariably have many mentors at different stages of our growth and development. Foundational values and character are formed in an early stage in life. For this reason, early mentoring can have a profound impact on the trajectories of children and adolescents. As with mythological stories and classical movies, we are guided by mentors but we fight the fight ourselves and, finally, pass on to our mentees the benefits of those lessons we got from our mentors and our own experience. K. V. Dinesha gives us an example of this in Sidebar 3.1 on page 55.

With that in mind, let's review some of the changes adolescents undergo before and during the mentoring experience.

Early Adolescence

Early adolescence is the age beginning at approximately 10 or 11 years old and merging with mid adolescence at age 14 or 15. This is a time of great physical, intellectual, social and emotional growth. Physically, the young girls' growth will begin and peak much earlier than the boys' growth pattern. Reproductive systems begin to develop and secondary sex characteristics will also begin to develop.

Intellectually, children will begin exploring more abstract thinking, as they begin conducting "formal operations" of "what might be true if?" scenarios rather than their previous concrete thinking about "What is?" In this stage, children will not always be able to perceive the long-range implications of their current decision-making. Their interests will expand, and as they do so they will experience intense, short-term enthusiasm over their new discoveries.

Socially and emotionally children at this stage tend to turn inward as they become more self-aware. They will become preoccupied with their rapid body changes, drawing into themselves to become more self-absorbed and self-conscious. Children may also experience diminished self-esteem in this stage of growth.

Early adolescents will begin redefining relationships with their family at this stage. While they will continue to look to the family for guidance and values, they will move toward increased independence. At this stage of growth parents will encounter "skirmishes," but few major conflicts concerning parental control.

Peers will take on an increasingly significant importance in children's lives at this stage. The children will seek to become part of a group as they compare their own normality and acceptance with same-sex peers. Being part of a group will help them hide their insecurities as a result of their rapid changes. During this time they will also move toward more intimate sharing of their feelings with their peers.

At this stage, the children will begin exploring and understanding sexuality by defining themselves in terms of maleness and femaleness. This is an important stage in which they begin to learn how to relate to the opposite sex.

Middle Adolescence

During middle adolescence, which begins around age 14 or 15 and continues on through the beginnings of late adolescence at age 17, physical, intellectual social and emotional growth will rapidly continue. Physically, their growth rate will peak and then begin slowing as their stature reaches approximately 95% of their adult height in this stage. Maturity and secondary sex characteristics will be well advanced by the end of this stage.

Intellectually, students will demonstrate growing competence in abstract thinking. They will be capable of perceiving future implications of current actions and decisions, but these may not always apply to them, as they will understand what the potential results of their actions will be, but may still take actions concerning themselves and their activities in which, in their minds the repercussions to themselves are nonexistent. Under stressful conditions their minds will revert to the concrete thinking process, closing themselves off from analysis of potential risks.

Socially and emotionally, children at this stage may have pre-occupations with fantasy worlds and idealism as their abstract thinking and a sense of future develops. They will also begin reestablishing their own body image as their growth rates slow.

During this stage, the previous "skirmishes" may turn into "all-out warfare" as the children test their limits concerning parental controls. No household rule will go untested. Major conflicts will erupt as the children struggle for parental emancipation and greater autonomy in their own lives. Based upon their intellectual and emotional stages, the child's push for greater autonomy may also provide fertile ground for dangerous and potentially harmful behaviors.

In this stage, student cliques will be formed as the adolescence begin strongly identifying with chosen peers to affirm their self-image. In addition, they will begin looking to peers rather than parents or other role models for behavioral codes. The adolescent sexuality will expand as they begin to test their ability to attract others to them and continue to explore the parameters of masculinity and femininity. This stage also becomes formative in developing sexual codes of behavior, as well as an embedded personal value system.

INFLUENCES

To be an effective mentor is imperative that the mentor understand the environment of the mentee in physical, cultural and familial terms, in addition to the typical behaviors and pressures their mentee's face. Research has identified several key influences of youth behavior to which the mentor must be attuned. Program training sessions and conversations with other mentors will help expand each of these topic areas as they relate to your mentee and their environment.

Family economic realities often make it difficult for poor youth to perform well in school (Wiley). Students may also shy away from establishing relationships with other students and/or the mentor. Students may have difficulty trusting those around them, especially adults. Sidebar 3.2 on page 60 shows how important peer relationships are for adolescents and teenagers, and even young adults. Sanghamitra Bandyopadhyay's anecdote also points out the importance of inculcating perseverance as a habit from an early age. Another point this anecdote makes is to not stop trying for fear of failure. Instead, give it your best effort and, if unsuccessful accept the outcome and try again with different preparation or a different way.

In some cases, a mentee may project a feeling of hopelessness about their future, and display cynical behaviors. These are characteristics indicative of student coping mechanisms due to the stress of poverty. Mentors must be aware of these characteristics and be prepared to expend additional time in developing strong relationships with these mentees.

WARNING SIGNS

It is important to be aware of some of the warning signs mentees may exhibit, which can provide indicators on specific behavioral problems or changes. Pay close attention to these and recommend intervention by experts in the areas as soon as the warning signs are noted.

Substance Abuse

Substance abuse is a serious problem in our modern society. This includes tobacco, drugs and alcohol. While cigarette smoking is declining among males, the female smoking population continues to grow. A multitude of drugs are available in our local communities today and it is rare that a student has not experimented with drugs in some fashion, including use of home chemicals. The most prevalent intoxicant of choice for youth continues to

Sidebar 3.2. If you don't try you have already failed

Prof. Sanghamitra Bandyopadhyay, Director
Indian Statistical Institute, Kolkata, India

From a very young age, my mother acted as my mentor. I was encouraged to climb trees, ride bicycles, participate in dramatics and musical programs, drive cars, and what not. Once when I was feeling apprehensive about climbing a tree my mother assured me: "Don't worry, climb. I am standing below. If you fall, I will catch you."

I remember her words often. I soared with the faith that if I fell my "Ma" would catch me. She was there. Today my mother is suffering from dementia, bedridden for more than two years and often looks at me blankly, and I say to myself, "Why did you give up Ma? Could I not hold you tightly enough?"

In my school days, I was never at the top of my class. I was not very ambitious, but always gave it my best effort in whatever I did, and I'd be happy with whatever the result was with few regrets. I always lived in the present, hardly dwelt on the past, and gave scant thought to the future. I was never extremely happy nor depressed.

Looking back, I realize now that this was probably a subconscious reaction to the fact my family moved frequently as my father held a transferable job. This resulted in a number of school changes, and leaving old friends behind was always painful. Every time we moved, I was almost certain that I would not survive the separation from my friends, from my school. And each time I was surprised to find myself adjusting to the new environment, making new friends. The old friends whom I had promised to always keep in touch with were slowly forgotten.

This probably shaped my character to a large extent. I could not afford to be depressed for long periods over lost friends, or I'd be depressed every few years. Today I take life as it comes: I'm happy if I succeed, and I'm not too badly off if I don't.

Once in college my mentor, who would eventually become my husband, was a strict task master, much stricter than I was with myself. He was the driving force behind many of my achievements. But for his encouragement and guidance, I would not have even attempted many things. A firm believer in never giving up despite all odds, he has driven me to attain more than I ever thought myself capable of. And that's the mark of a good mentor.

Another mentor, my PhD supervisor where I did my postgraduate coursework in computer science, played a major role in my academic make-up. The challenging environment and program taught me the value of hard work and to enjoy every bit of it. Being a well-decorated scientist himself, he made getting a "Bhatnagar award," a prestigious prize given yearly to the most outstanding scientists in India, sound so normal that many of his students, including me, gained the

If you don't try you have already failed (continued)

confidence and will to aim for it. I have always felt that most Indian students, especially girls, suffer from a lack of confidence and self-esteem that holds them back from trying many things. It is important to have faith on one's abilities and to accept that "if others can do it, then I can too."

In turn, I have tried to mentor my students as well as my son in the way I was mentored. Times and outlooks have changed. Sometimes I have succeeded, sometimes I have failed. But I hope I have been able to pass on these lessons:

First, it's okay to fail, and it's normal to not always get what you want, or what you think you deserve, but it is not okay to give up without trying. If you try you may fail, if you do not try you have already failed.

Second, remember your good times as well as your bad times as neither will last forever. Do your best, do not turn away from opportunities and challenges that come your way, have the courage to move into uncharted territory—and then accept the outcome. The only important thing is that you should not be found wanting in your effort.

Above all, always remain a good and kind human being. And behind every successful person there is a mentor, often more than one.

be alcohol. Mentors must be aware of the various forms and indicators of substance abuse when dealing with their mentees. This is an opportunity for mentors to also demonstrate strength as a role model for the students.

Injuries and Violence

Accidents are the leading cause of death for 15 to 21-year-olds, with automobile accidents accounting for most of these deaths, and in the majority of cases drivers are under the influence of alcohol as well.

Males in this age group are frequently victims and/or perpetrators of crimes. Since this is a time where students become more associated with peers, are testing their masculinity and looking to their peers for approval, a mob or gang mentality may quickly develop, escalating into street crimes and attacks on other students. These group behaviors can have significant impacts on both participants and bystanders. Student bystanders may fear these activities and, as a result curtail their own extra-curricular activities in the evenings.

This type of violence spreads quickly from the street and neighborhood into the school environment. Mentors, especially those who are teachers or professors at universities must pay particular attention to the spread of these activities on school grounds.

Suicide

Since it is often difficult for youth to express their failure and feelings, especially feelings of depression to adults, and particularly to their parents, suicide has become the second leading cause of death for youth. In addition to the normal growth stresses associated with this age group, additional stress from family and others pertaining to academic performance may be a significant factor with which the students are unprepared to deal effectively, resulting in thoughts of suicide.

Adolescents may also be reluctant to share information and their concerns about other friends who may be having suicidal thoughts. Mentors must have the discernment to understand when the pressures on their mentees may be too great, and must constantly assess changes in mentee behavior. It is only through experience that a mentor can discern the appropriate pressure that a mentee can handle. In all cases, it is useful that the mentors focus on building skills among the mentees to set their targets.

Peer Pressure

Approval from peers is very important to adolescents. It is often difficult for youth to understand that peer influence decisions can have a lifelong consequence. Mentors must be prepared to help their mentees develop effective problem-solving skills and life skills, to be able to appropriately cope with the sense of their own competence and responsibility in dealing with their problems individually rather than through the influence of their peers.

Technology and Cyber Bullying

Today's youth have never known a world in which they could not maintain constant contact with their friends through social media. Computers, cell phones and a multitude of other electronic devices have enabled them to maintain communications through text messages, emails, and other applications, including Facebook and Twitter.

> … [C]yber bullying can be an even more brutal and destructive force than the harassment that occurs on the schoolyard, as [it is] ever present …

It's important for mentors to emphasize the importance of face-to-face social interactions and development of other basic social and communication skills. Mentors should also discuss the importance of information posted by their mentees to the World Wide Web. Once the information is out there, it is permanently out there. There is no way to take the information back and serious repercussions in their social lives as well as their careers may follow them for many years.

These wonderful devices that enable us to be connected and communicate constantly have also enabled bullying to become a pervasive activity in all aspects of a student's life. Electronic taunting, teasing and harassing continues to follow the student wherever their electronic lives may lead them.

Researchers have discovered that cyber bullying can be an even more brutal and destructive force than the harassment that occurs on the schoolyard, as this ever present threat invades every activity. In many cases, computers are hacked and student passwords and electronic identities are stolen, only to appear in some later form of harassment.

Mentors must take cyber bullying as a serious threat to their mentee. If your mentee identifies himself as a victim of cyber bullying, take it seriously and share the information with program staff and the mentees family members. It is also key for mentors to stress the importance of not participating in cyber bullying, as well as identifying those who may be victims.

POTENTIAL INDICATORS OF TROUBLE

A mentor should be aware of the multiple warning signs that mentees may be having problems. Pay attention to the following warning signs (Wiley) indicating an adolescent may need outside help:

Suicide
- Giving away possessions
- Making a will
- Talking about death or dying
- Prolonged depression
- Saying his/her family would be better off without him/her
- Being suddenly quiet, withdrawn, or at peace may indicate a decision to end the pain by ending life.
- Evidence of a plan and method

Drug or alcohol abuse
- Irrational or "spaced out" behavior
- A sudden increase in accidents
- Lying

- Loss of interest in school
- Secretiveness
- Spending a lot of time alone
- Severe mood swings
- Alcohol on breath
- Sleeping a lot

Physical abuse, sexual abuse, neglect (including incest)
- Non-accidental physical injury
- Frequent "accidents"
- Abrupt changes in personality
- Withdrawal
- Physical defensiveness
- Running away
- Sudden onset of compulsive and/or self-destructive behavior
- Reluctance to be with a particular family member

Other warning signs
- Major weight loss
- Poor self-image
- Problems at school
- Serious depression
- Law-breaking behavior

LET'S TALK

Each generation develops their own way of communicating with their peers. Add to this formula development of slang phrases which reflect common youth cultures and our own penchant to develop our "industry" languages, specific to particular occupations, and a mentor may feel their mentee is speaking in a foreign tongue as we try to communicate to one another. This is not unusual. Mentors may need to develop their own "dictionary" of current expressions that mentees may be using.

In the same regard, it is important for mentors to express their experiences in ways that the mentees will understand. An important first part will be using your dictionary of expressions to help you explain these important lessons in your life. Keep in mind, the same word may have completely different meanings depending on the changing time and context of the situation, as well as the inflection of voice. It may be beneficial to refer to current online definitions of common words and expressions, such as those presented in The Urban Dictionary.

Mentors can work with their mentees to develop a common language of expression. This may take some time, but will be a result of constant communication with your mentee. Remember that your mentee may not be able to express himself/herself in the same way that you expect. Work hard in this aspect to understand.

This may also be an opportune moment to discuss transactional analysis and the effects of both the sender of the message and the receiver of the message.

Transactional Analysis

We may recall, communication requires two people—a sender and receiver. How a sender prepares the message is just as important as the receiver's attitude on reception of the message. Transactional analysis was developed in 1957 by Eric Berne as a means of understanding behavior, and it was initially designed as a psychoanalytic theory and method of therapy to analyze and understand social transactions and determine the "ego state" of a patient. However, it also provides an excellent means for understanding a "point of view" in communications, and offers an opportunity for mentors and mentees to speak on a common level (Harrigan).

The basic philosophy behind transactional analysis is to reach a state of communication in which each person accepts the other person as having validity, importance, and equality

Figure 3.1. Ego states of a conversation

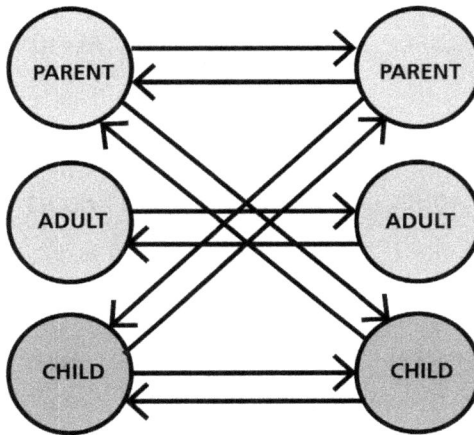

of respect. Positive reinforcement is an essential component in increasing an emotional state of acceptance of each other within the communication.

In our communications, both the mentor and mentee must have a desire for positive growth, and accept that each other has the capacity to think and has positive, important elements to discuss. Communication must be a two-way process in which there is no room for emotional obstacles.

Every conversation starts as a reflection of the individual psyche represented as one of three ego states in which we both send information and receive information (Figure 3.1). These three ego states are;

Parent. In this state, individuals will emotionally feel, think and behave in a manner reflecting how a parent or authoritarian figure would act or respond to a child or subordinate respectively.

Adult. In the adult ego state, the communicator or receiver acts logically and objectively to the message being presented. There

Figure 3.2. Examples of cross communication

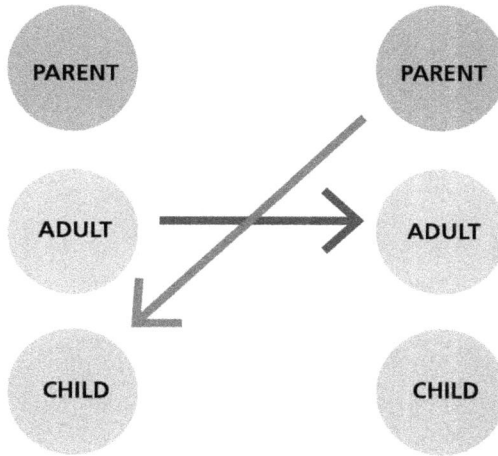

are no hidden agendas and information is exchanged on the level it is presented, that is, as information.

Child. The child is an ego state in which people will behave, feel and think similar to a child by receiving information or responding to information emotionally. This can take the form of scolding, or praising.

In our conversations we may unknowingly approach the conversation from one of these ego states. In a normal conversation, we make go in and out of each of the states both as receivers of the information as well as senders of the information.

The goal of mentors is to speak to mentees in an overall adult-to-adult model, as shown in Figure 3.1. When the lines are crossed, mentors and mentees may find their communications become ineffective, as Figure 3.2 illustrates.

Mentors may find themselves as the obvious authority figure in a conversation with mentees. However, the goal is to communicate effectively with mentees. If, as a mentor, you place yourself in a parent-to-child reference point, your mentee may perceive that you have a lack of respect for them, a limited view of their world and an inability to understand their point of view. In this transaction, they may respond back to you as a child, as if you are scolding them or preaching to them rather than communicating with them at an equal level.

The goal of your conversation is to demonstrate your respect of the mentee, their values and points of view as well as their potential limited experience, raise them up to the adult level, and communicate to them as if you are communicating to another mentor to explain your life experiences and lessons learned.

By communicating in this fashion you will be able to effectively exchange information, and open yourself up to opportunities to more fully understand and assist your mentee.

By the same token, the mentee must have the mindset where they are learning as an adult, that they are not being talked down to, lectured to, nor scolded, but rather being asked to take responsibility to evaluate the information presented in a more open, unemotional state.

How Am I Perceived?

It's been said, "You have only one chance to make a good impression." One of the objectives of the mentoring program is to make sure that mentees are always perceived as educated, serious students, and professionals. Perceptions go both ways. As you evaluate your mentee, so does your mentee evaluate you!

You need to know your mentee and some of the many popular influences around them. Taking some time to share their interests will help you better understand and relate to the mentees, helping to build a bond in the relationship. This will also aid in developing better communications and avoid the negative "Parent-to-Child"/"Mentor-to-Protégé" communication that can destroy a mentor-protégé relationship before it even begins.

KEY POINTS ABOUT MENTORING YOUTHS

In this chapter we discussed the particular stresses and issues that youthful mentees experience during their physical, intellectual, social, and emotional development. Following are key points to remember about mentees in this age group:

1. Mentoring in all stages of life from pre-K though our professional lives leads to better academic and professional performance, better school and work attendance and all-around positive attitudes in life.

2. A successful role model-mentor understands the role learning plays in each stage of their protégés' lives, then develops successful strategies for their mentees that are age and life appropriate.

3. Outside influences can play a significant role both positively and negatively in a protégés life. Mentors must be attuned to potential negative influences in their mentees.

4. Advances in technology and the proliferation of electronic devices have also led to cyber bullying, sexting, or other harmful influences. Mentors must be attuned to these influences and take them seriously, reporting them to family and law enforcement officials where and when appropriate.

5. Transactional analysis allows us to better see how we are communicating with our protégés and to improve our ability to communicate with others.

CHAPTER

4

Learning and the Mind

Education is not the learning of facts, but the
training of the mind to think.

—Albert Einstein

ONLY RECENTLY HAVE we been able to understand the human mind—how we really think and learn, and ultimately how we can impart information to build knowledge successfully to others. We are in the midst of an extraordinary growth of scientific research work on the human mind and brain as well as the processes of thinking and learning.

Over the last four decades as these revolutionary research studies have borne fruit, we are cultivating further seeds to develop revolutionary new insights into education and learning. New theories of learning are coming into focus every day which lead to different approaches in the design of educational curriculum, teaching methods, and educational assessments. Let's first examine what learning is.

WHAT IS LEARNING?

John B. Watson, an American psychologist who popularized the scientific theory of behaviorism, said about learning in his book, *Behaviorism,*

> ... all schools of psychology except that of behaviorism claim that *consciousness* is the subject-matter of psychology. Behaviorism, on the contrary, holds that the subject matter of human psychology is the behavior or activities of the human being. Behaviorism claims that consciousness is neither a definable nor a usable concept; that it is merely another word for the *soul* of more ancient times. The old psychology is thus dominated by a kind of subtle religious philosophy.*

Since then, the growth in interdisciplinary research results are enabling cognitive researchers to better understand and work with teachers to develop different learning environments and classroom interactions to enhance our students learning experience.

Constructivism

One of the emerging learning theories is *constructivism* where students are active learners engaged in constructing knowledge rooted in previous experience, rather than only through lectures or readings. This process is facilitated through hands-on projects and interactions between teacher, mentor and student for a stronger, deeper learning experience, as Beth Klein points out in Sidebar 4.1 on page 74. The use of technology in the learning experience also helps students to visualize and bring to life educational concepts.

The experience with learning is far richer today than ever

---

* Many of the principles outlined in this chapter are discussed and adapted from the Committee on Developments in the Science of Learning (2000).

before, and promises to evolve dramatically within the next few generations. As mentors, we must be prepared to adapt new learning methodologies that will improve our ability to pass on our life experiences to our mentees. This will require that as mentors we adopt a mentoring mindset.

[E]merging learning styles ... move the learning experience from a lecture or reading only experience to ... students ... mentor[,] and teacher interactions [to] facilitate a ... deeper learning experience.

Over the last three or four decades there has been an explosion in the study of the human mind and our capacity to learn. New theories of learning are evolving every day that lead us to examine different approaches to the design of curriculum, teaching, and assessments than those we may have experienced in the past.

The advancement in learning theories has also opened up the growth of interdisciplinary inquiries about the human mind and the human capacity for learning.

Perhaps more importantly, today's research is leading to significant improvements in the classroom. Educators are actively seeking new information from researchers in the field of cognitive science to improve their teaching strategies, assessment techniques and student learning outcomes.

The experience goes hand-in-hand with cognitive scientists and researchers who are now spending more time working with teachers in order to test and refine emerging theories under actual classroom conditions. This enables the scientist to understand how different settings and classroom interactions are actually influencing application of their theories.

Sidebar 4.1. From "I can't" to "I got it"

Dr. Beth Klein, Reading Interventionist
Reading Portal, L.L.C., South Florida, U.S.A.

The majority of my career has been as a clinical psychologist, but recently I started an educational practice as a teacher/interventionist/mentor, helping students with reading problems to better prepare them for educational challenges ahead. I've observed that oftentimes my students with academic issues have an emotional and/or behavioral component and are otherwise bright.

One such student was Dani. When I first met her, she presented as highly verbal and curious. She easily engaged in conversation and was animated and enthusiastic—until I asked her to read—and her demeanor changed completely. Dani became much quieter and withdrew into herself, and nearly whispered, "I'm not very smart. The other kids in my class are all able to read but I never could."

Dani had tested as a highly intelligent young girl but her reading, spelling, and writing skills hovered around the 5th percentile. In other words, 95% of students her age performed higher than her in literacy skills. She faced her severe difficulty every single day in school, which made her feel "dumb," even though her intelligence and language testing indicated she was quite bright.

"Dani, I want you know that many kids struggle with reading and writing; it's actually much more common than you might think." I paused, then continued,

"And your testing results show that you're really smart!"

Her facial expression told me that she wasn't buying this. "If I'm so smart, why do I keep getting really low grades on most of my schoolwork?"she said sadly. When I asked her what she felt good at, she replied "I'm really good at math, one of the highest in the class, except I can't do word problems."

That her only shortcoming in math was word problems was one of the telltale signs of dyslexia. When I pointed out her very high math test scores her face brightened and betrayed a smile. "Word problems are going to get easier for you as your reading improves," I said as I handed Dani a letter-tile board where we built words sound-by-sound with simple words. With a little guidance, she did beautifully and was willing to try slightly harder words.

Dani loved playful games, so I incorporated literacy video games that felt light and fun but were actually quite content-laden. I chose games that reinforced the current lessons she was learning.

Over time, with evidence-based instruction and encouragement, Dani's reading and writing skills greatly improved, and she felt increasingly motivated and capable. By using learned strategies, she was able to apply her new decoding skills to increasingly challenging multi-syllable words. Among the many exercises

From "I can't" to "I got it" (continued)

was choral reading, where I read a paragraph, then she read a paragraph. Soon, she began saying "I got this" more and more as she wanted to read it all on her own.

Dani's literacy skills have significantly improved with reading/writing intervention, to the degree that she was taken out of small group intervention in school, and she currently receives all As in her classes without any additional classroom assistance. As a result, her self-esteem is greatly improved and she has a very promising academic future ahead as a result of teaching/mentoring.

Kids will be more willing to engage in learning when they are made aware of their strengths, when they are encouraged to believe they'll be able to improve their areas of weakness, when they are guided toward successful experiences, when they become more comfortable making mistakes, and when their natural curiosity is nurtured.

Other Approaches

A variety of research approaches and techniques have already been developed and others are underway. Nearly all of these approaches and techniques have been developed through evidence-based research in a variety of sciences. The scientific convergence in education and learning is providing far more fertile grounds for advanced educational and learning research, which promises to evolve dramatically in the next generation.

Today we know far more than we did only a few years ago. Cognitive psychology research has provided an increased understanding of the nature of competent performance in the principles of knowledge organization that underlie human abilities to solve problems in mathematics, science, literature, social studies and history (Committee).

Through the work of developmental research educators are seeing a greater understanding by young children of the basic principles of biology and physical causality, as well as their understanding of number, narrative and personal intent, making it possible to create innovative curricula that introduce important concepts for advanced reasoning at early ages (ibid).

Research in learning has unveiled many important principles for structuring new learning experiences enabling people to apply what they have learned in new settings. Additionally, social psychology, cognitive psychology, and anthropology have demonstrated that learning takes place in settings where cultural and social norms as well as expectations influence learning and transfer of information in significant ways. Neuroscience is coming-of-age by providing evidence for many learning principles that had previously emerged in laboratory research. Scientists as well as educators are now understanding how learning changes the physical structure of the brain, as well as the functional organization of the brain (ibid).

Using these types of collaborative research studies—which are "lessons in inter-disciplinarity, the ability to work with several disciplines for better results..." (see Sidebar 4.2)—educators and scientists are now working to design and evaluate learning environments in multiple settings, as well as incorporating the vast "wisdom of practice" demonstrated by successful teachers and mentors who are sharing their experiences and expertise. Combined with emerging technologies, educators and mentors are opening vast opportunities to guide and enhance student learning (ibid).

No longer are we focused solely on the acquisition of literacy skills, the three "Rs" of reading, writing and arithmetic. Educational systems are now training people to think and read critically, while expressing themselves clearly and persuasively. Scientists and engineers are being taught to solve complex problems in science, engineering and math using logic, new techniques and critical thinking—all critical skills for nearly everyone living today's contemporary lifestyles.

Workforce skills for this new generation have changed significantly and educators worldwide are responding to provide competitive workers for the next generation in science, technology, engineering, math and the arts. As a result of the enormous

Sidebar 4.2. Crises (and mistakes) are learning opportunities

AMARESH CHAKRABARTI. SENIOR PROFESSOR & CHAIR
Department of Design and Manufacture, Indian Institute of Science, Bengaluru

Lessons in inter-disciplinarity, the ability to work with several disciplines for better results, grew strongest in the hands of Dr. Thomas P. Bligh, my PhD supervisor at Cambridge University. Tom, as he preferred to be called, had a master's in mechanical engineering and a PhD in physics and first worked for an oil company designing underwater dredgers, before joining the University of Minnesota as an Assistant Professor in both Civil and Mechanical Engineering. At Minnesota, he designed solar collectors as well as the Civil Engineering building of the university that in 1983 he won the American Society of Civil Engineers' award for the most environmentally sustainable building in the U.S.A.!

Tom was subsequently poached by the Massachusetts Institute of Technology where he initiated its first Innovation Center before being head-hunted by Cambridge University, where I got to work under him for a PhD

Tom did his PhD under Sir Frank Nabarro, whose academic lineage went on one hand to Sir Issac Newton and Galileo Galilei, and on the other to Charles Darwin. Tom served on the same committee as Richard Feynman to investigate the Challenger disaster, and an entrepreneur who invented a bio-colony picking device that went on to become a major tool in the Human-Genome project, catapulting his company to one of the fastest growing in the U.K. and making him a millionaire.

He taught me the importance of hands on skills. His personal workshop was as big as that in my department, and he could use every tool, from machining to woodworking, with virtuosity, better than most mechanics did at his department! "How would you know the potential of a product if you cannot make it yourself?" he would say. His knowledge of materials and manufacturing was deep, and his curiosity without limit!

On his curiosity, let me share a story. Scholarships were running out as I was trying desperately to finish my PhD at Cambridge. With little resources, all I could afford was a tiny room in a shared house. One night I stayed away, and when I returned I was aghast to find that a large, heavy chunk of the ceiling had fallen on my bed. Had I spent that night in my bed, I would have been crushed! Horrified, I narrated the accident to Tom. His response?: "That's terrible, but did you examine the structure of its failure mechanism? It was a rare opportunity to see those!"

amount of information and knowledge being created today learning everything is an impossibility.

Today's educational goal is better thought of as enabling

students to develop intellectual skills and learning strategies needed to acquire knowledge to think productively and profoundly, as well as understanding where information and knowledge can be gained. More than ever the world requires self-sustained, lifelong learners capable of discerning fact from fiction.

New approaches will continue to develop. Educators and mentors must also understand the advanced educational theories and practices and adapt new ways to introduce students to traditional subjects and life experiences.

HOW WE LEARN

The science of learning began through the study of philosophy and theology and, by the early 1900s, research studies had ushered in the new school of behaviorism, focusing on the scientific study of observable behaviors and stimulus conditions that control them. Early behaviorists conceptualized learning as a process of forming connections between stimuli and responses, while motivation was relegated to the role of a primary "drive," like hunger, thirst or other external forces such as rewards and punishments (ibid).

Since behaviorism focused on observable stimulus conditions and associated behaviors, the concepts of *understanding, reasoning,* and *thinking*, which today we consider of paramount importance for education, could not be adequately investigated. Slowly, the science advanced to the use of behavior as data, but allowed for hypothesis concerning internal "mental states" which could be used to explain various phenomena.

As the complexity of understanding humans and their environments became increasingly apparent, the field of *cognitive science* emerged. Approaching learning from a multidisciplinary perspective, cognitive science melds research data from anthropology, linguistics, philosophy, developmental psychology, computer science, neuroscience, and several branches of psychology

(Committee). Today we are learning from new experimental tools, methodologies and ways of postulating theories which have made it possible for scientists to delve more deeply into mental functioning, testing their theories rather than simply speculating about thinking and learning (ibid).

Mentors and educators need to understand one of the primary characteristics of the new science of learning, that is, it focuses on the processes of knowing.

Knowing and Pre-existing Knowledge

As infants, humans are already active learners in that our brains give precedence to certain kinds of information such as language, basic concepts of numbers, physical properties, and the movement of animate and inanimate objects. By separating the stimuli infants are capable of constructing new knowledge and understanding.

As we continue the education process we can construct new knowledge from our existing knowledge. Teachers have been building on these ideas for years by filling in the blanks of our incomplete understandings, false beliefs and naïve renditions of concepts. As our knowledge base rounds out, each student is able to achieve a more mature understanding of the world. Mentors and educators need to be aware of students preconceived ideas based upon their knowledge of their environment, which may not be based upon the scientific explanations of these phenomena.

From this understanding we derive two paths for an educational experience. We can allow students to construct knowledge for themselves through our direction and opportunities to participate in new experiences, such as that gained by hands-on experiences and project-based learning. A secondary method, and one upon which nearly all educational systems have been based, is one in which we experience "teaching by telling" (ibid).

New research indicates significant evidence that student learning experiences or combinations of these two methodologies
where learning is enhanced when educators pay attention to the
knowledge and beliefs learners bring with them. Using student
pre-existing knowledge as a foundation, educators can expand
student understanding through both guided discussions and lectures, as well as hands-on experiences.

Active Learning

Learning and understanding are activities that go hand-in-
hand. As people learn, they must also recognize when they completely understand or if they need additional information. In
other words, people must have the motivation to continuously
explore and expand their knowledge base. The process of students seeking additional strategies for understanding and building their own theories, as well as the capacity to test them effectively is known as active learning.

… students … [can] construct knowledge
… by hands-on experiences and project-
based learning … [or by] "teaching by
telling"…

An important component of active learning is *metacognition*,
which refers to the ability to predict one's own performance
on various tasks and to monitor current levels of mastery and
understanding. Teachers and mentors can enhance the metacognitive approach to learning by including approaches that
focus on sense making, self-assessment and reflection on how
success was achieved, and perhaps more importantly what can

be learned from failures.

When students apply these practices, research has shown that students can greatly increase the degree to which they can transfer their learning to new settings and events.

The active learning approach incorporates student learning by teaching other students within the small group atmosphere. In these environments, teachers and mentors provide information prior to the lesson, then spend time supervising groups as the students work among themselves. This is a hands-on activity for teachers and mentors as they focus on the groups to ensure that all students are engaged, that each is participating fairly and equally and that the group activity is producing quality products. In addition, active learning teachers and mentors will be attentive to what the students are learning through their experience in the learning process, as well as the group's productivity.

As mentors and an active learning process is important to recognize how the learning activity was conceived. Did it start as a mentor introduced project, or did it emerge from the student's own knowledge and building effort? Significant differences can be achieved when active learning is incorporated into teacher and mentor introduced learning activities.

In these activities the greater portion of the teacher's and mentor's work will be done before the group activity is even conceived and carried out. It will be the students themselves, and their motivation to continue exploring and learning that drives the active learning process.

Mentors and teachers must inspire the students to develop activities which will enhance their learning. Then, teachers and mentors must be available, and aware of how the students are learning and applying their experiences within group activities and the learning process to better facilitate learning outcomes.

Active learning requires a new mindset from teachers, mentors and their students. Each must be prepared to assist in the student process of self-motivation as students seek to understand complex subject matter and transfer what they have learned into new problems and settings. As we adapt these new methodologies we must ourselves become active learners to more fully understand: (1) memory and the structure of knowledge; (2) problem solving and reasoning; (3) the early foundations of learning; (4) regulatory processes that govern learning, including metacognition; and (5) how symbolic thinking emerges from the culture and community of the learner (ibid).

KEY LEARNING FACTS

As mentors it is important for us to understand three key facts upon which to base our mentoring experience and assist us in understanding, communicating and teaching our mentees.

Students come to the classroom with preconceptions about how the world works. If these initial understandings are not understood and engaged, mentees may fail to grasp new concepts and information. In many cases, students whose preconceptions are not questioned and examined, may learn new items but will quickly forget the, reverting to their preconceptions outside the classroom. Children will begin in preschool years to develop processes to make sense of the world around them. Initial understandings can have a powerful effect on the integration of new concepts and information (ibid).

… to gain a deeper understanding of a subject [mentees] need to use a *conceptual framework*, the set of key abstract ideas, constructs or measurable factors that are principal to the subject under study …

While these initial understandings provide a solid foundation upon which to learn, occasionally the understandings are inaccurate. These misconceptions can affect a student's understanding of science if the physical properties cannot be easily observed. The same holds true for humanities, where preconceptions often include stereotypes or simplifications. Effective teaching elicits from students pre-existing understanding of the subjects and provides opportunities upon which to build or challenge initial understandings (ibid).

Mentees must understand that to gain a deeper understanding of a subject they need to use a *conceptual framework*, the set of key abstract ideas, constructs or measurable factors that are principal to the subject under study; and mentors must constantly seek these existing preconceptions within their mentees to assist in building new models upon which the mentees can understand more complex problems and rewrite misconceptions into formidable knowledge.

To develop competence in an area, students must:

- have a deep foundation of factual knowledge,

- understand facts and ideas in the context of the conceptual framework, and

- organize knowledge in ways that facilitate retrieval and application.

A body of research exists that compares the performance of "experts" and "novices" on learning and learning transfer. Regardless of their field of expertise, or whether they are considered "good thinkers" or "smart people," experts always draw upon a richly structured information base. Within this foundation, they have acquired the ability to plan a task, to notice patterns, to generate reasonable arguments and explanations, and to draw analogies to other problems.

More importantly, these experts have experienced learning as a process for deeper understanding, enabling them to transform information into usable knowledge. Unlike novices, the expert's comprehensive understanding of multiple concepts enables them to shape their understanding of new information by quickly seeing emerging patterns, relationships or discrepancies that may not be apparent to others (ibid).

In the formal education process, students begin as novices then quickly move in the direction of acquiring additional information and deeper understanding to provide greater expertise. This requires both a deepening of the information base and development of a conceptual framework upon which the subject matter is based (ibid).

Organizing information into conceptual frameworks allows for greater transfer of information. The conceptual framework provides "hangers" upon which new information can be attached, quickly recalled and reassessed as additional information is acquired. As concepts are reinforced, students naturally gain the capacity to transfer learning beyond the classroom through their own observation and inquiry.

Students will seize the opportunity to take control of their own learning when they are taught the metacognitive approach to instruction.

Experts are masters at monitoring their own understanding. They make note of the need for additional information when required, and are quickly able to synthesize new information, determining if this information is consistent with what they have already learned and what analogies could be drawn that will advance their understanding. This use of metacognitive monitoring activities are an important element of *adaptive expertise* (ibid).

Experts also have developed their own internal conversation, or dialogue enabling them to quickly compare, sort and analyze new information. As mentors it will be important to analyze the mentee's capacity to predict outcomes and assist them in developing strategies to improve their internal dialogue and consequently improve their understanding.

■ ■ ■

KEY POINTS ABOUT LEARNING AND THE MIND

In this chapter we examined what learning is, and the various ways that the human mind absorbs information. Following are key points for mentors and mentees to remember about learning and the mind:

1. Learning requires different environments and interactions to enhance the student experience.

2. There are several theories of learning that have provided revolutionary insights into education and learning, including behaviorism, constructivism, and developmental learning.

3. The science of learning evolved from early studies in philosophy, theology and psychology.

4. Cognitive science now approaches learning from a multidisciplinary perspective melding research data from anthropology, linguistics, philosophy, developmental psychology, computer science, neuroscience and many other branches of science.

5. Educational and learning experiences derive from one of two paths; "hands-on experiences," known as active learning, or "teaching by telling."

6. Mentors must understand three key facts of learning since students base new learning on their pre-existing understanding; if their knowledge is incorrect, it must be corrected

before they can continue to build new learning models.

- Students must have a deep foundational, factual knowledge upon which to base new learning. Students misunderstand new facts and ideas in the context of the conceptual framework they have already established.

- Students must organize knowledge in ways that facilitate retrieval and application.

CHAPTER

5

The Mentoring Mindset

Whether you think you can or you think you can't,
you're right.

—Henry Ford

BASED UPON OUR understanding of recent research into learning, we can no longer think of students as "empty vessels ready to be filled with knowledge." Teachers and mentors must actively inquire into students' thinking, and provide learning environments and conditions upon which students' thinking can be sharpened. Using a student's initial conceptions as a baseline, mentors can effectively co-construct knowledge where the student is an active participant.

The traditional concept of lecture and testing is inadequate to develop tomorrow's great leaders and thinkers. Assessments must be developed to tap into understanding rather than require students to repeat facts or perform skills in isolation.

Teachers and mentors must take opportunities to learn how

to recognize predictable preconceptions of students that may interfere with their mastery of challenging subjects. They must also be experts in drawing out preconceptions that may not be predictable, and be able to work with and challenge these pre-conceptions so that children can build upon them or replace them when appropriate.

Additionally, teachers and mentors must teach their subject matter in depth, providing multiple examples which demon-strate the concepts in play and provide a firm foundation of factual knowledge.

In today's modern education there is no room for superficial coverage of topics. All topics must be discussed in sufficient detail to allow key concepts of the discipline to be understood. Case studies must be sufficient in number to allow students to grasp defining concepts, as well as identify those unique discrepancies upon which a sound analytical framework can be constructed.

LEARNING, THE MIND, AND OUR BRAINS

Each human mind is as unique as the individual to whom it belongs. While our brains may be physically similar in structure and areas involved in processing information, each one is unique in the way that it processes, stores and recalls information. By understanding how people learn we can formulate strategies to improve information presentation, resulting in improved learn-ing outcomes.

Focusing on how people learn helps mentors move beyond the basics of the lecture and evaluation approach of traditional education, and helps students understand and develop basic skills for thinking and problem-solving. Through activities asso-ciated with each lesson, students are more likely to find their own learning methodology and connect the why, when, and how of facts, as Sidebar 4.1 on page 74 illustrates.

Newly learned skills can be relevant to a wide variety of complex problems. Each student must be presented with a strong base of factual knowledge to promote complex problem-solving and support the transfer of knowledge into new student encounters.

Teachers and mentors who focus on how people learn must consider the many possible teaching strategies available to them and select the most appropriate style for their learners.

Based upon the learners in the group some teaching techniques may be better than others. The teaching methodologies must be chosen according to the task at hand. Each is a specialized tool that in the hand of the master teacher or mentor can provide wonderfully efficient ways of transmitting new information, obtaining extraordinary learning outcomes, exciting both the imagination and desire of our students to learn, while honing our students' critical skills.

It is, however the underlying student's preconceptions and levels of understanding that must be determined to monitor their learning outcome. There is no universal "best" teaching practice.

Incorporating learning methodologies and teaching strategies applies equally to learning for children as well as adult learning environments. Teachers and mentors must themselves understand, adopt and apply these methodologies and strategies.

Most educational organizations assume that work must be required to adapt and apply these methodologies and strategies for children, but when it comes to adult education and professional development programs, the programs are frequently not learner-centered to assist in the teacher or mentor growth.

These programs are often not knowledge-centered, instead simply introducing teachers and mentors to new techniques without providing opportunities to understand why, when, where and how these may be valuable in learning and teaching programs. The need to integrate structured activities with the curriculum content taught is especially important. Adult programs are also not usually assessment-centered.

Teachers and mentors incorporating new methodologies and strategies need open opportunities to incorporate these programs and then receive feedback about them. Teachers and mentors must develop their own knowledge through structured assessment programs in order to judge the success of transferring learning methodologies and strategies into classroom or teaching opportunities and their effects on student achievement.

> When solving problems, experts usually begin with trying to understand the problem rather than immediately inserting numbers or reaching for undeveloped solutions .... On the other hand, a novice tends ... to reach a solution without fully comprehending the problem.

As mentors, it is important for us to maintain relationships with our mentee. As professionals incorporating learning methodologies, it is also essential to maintain continued contact with other professionals and develop opportunities to discuss success and failure in our programs and mentoring relationships. To do so, teachers and mentors must maintain a community-centered approach, rather than working in isolation.

Learning and Transfer

When solving problems, experts usually begin with trying to understand the problem rather than immediately inserting numbers or reaching for undeveloped solutions. They quickly realize there may be additional components which may have been added or need to be applied to reach a solution to a problem. On the other hand, a novice tends to simply begin applying equations, or attempting to reach a solution without fully comprehending the problem.

In many respects adults and children approach problems much as experts and novices do. While adults apply their experience in dealing with a variety of problems to arrive at a solution, children may simply ask themselves, "which problem have I recently solved that looks similar?"

Novices, similar to children, often find they have no systematic way of making sense of contradictory information while problem-solving. They often lack the expert's deep understanding of how to interpret the problem and formulate a reasoned approach incorporating multiple experiences, solutions, and conflicting information. Ultimately, experts are able to organize their problem sets around big ideas, while breaking them down into smaller, solvable sub-problems.

Experts highlight the fact that "expert knowledge" is organized around important ideas and concepts. Similarly, teaching curricula must be organized in ways that lead to conceptual understanding.

Also, in many educational settings only superficial coverage of facts are presented before moving on to the next topic, leaving students little time to develop important, organizing ideas (Committee).

Retrieval of information by experts is also superior to that of novices, not because their memories are better but because they are conditioned to recognize when information is useful, enabling them to retrieve superior information concerning a specific problem (ibid).

Often, students solve sets of practice problems, basing their solutions on their knowledge of particular chapter concepts, rather than being able to apply an entire course of learning to the problems.

Expert Information Retrieval

A person's capacity to retrieve relevant information can vary from being *effortful* to relatively *effortless*, to *automatic* (Committee). These capacities demonstrate the characteristic of expertise, rather than the speed at which a task can be accomplished. For example, for any given problem an expert may be slower than a recently trained novice as the expert will attempt to fully understand the problem rather than jump immediately to a particular solution.

Often, students solve sets of practice problems, basing their solutions on their knowledge of particular chapter concepts, rather than being able to apply an entire course of learning to the problems.

There are several sub processes that occur within the overall process of problem solving. Many of these sub-processes place limited demands on conscious attention. Since the overall amount of information a person can attend to at any one time is limited (G. Miller), ease of processing some aspects of a task gives a person more capacity to attend to other, more intensive aspects of the problem.

In teaching, expertise can sometimes hamper the teaching experience, as experts may have forgotten what is easy and what is difficult for students at that specific stage of learning. Bear in mind the content knowledge necessary for expertise in the discipline needs to be differentiated from the pedagogical knowledge content underlying effective teaching (Committee). Pedagogical knowledge informs the teacher about typical difficulties students face in encountering the "learning" task, while content knowledge deals with detailed mastery and comprehension of the discipline at hand. Teachers and mentors must have expertise in these teaching areas in order to formulate the learning environment, as well as have expert knowledge of the field to understand the complexity of learning the discipline itself.

The implicit definition of an expert is, "someone who knows all the answers" which is usually *not* the case (Cognition "From Visual"; "Classroom"). The "expert" is more likely to be considered the "accomplished novice," a person skilled in a variety of areas, and of course proud of their accomplishments, but humble in realizing what they know is "minuscule compared to all that is potentially knowable" (Wiley).

Rather than having all of the answers, experts in this model, are free to continue learning despite having 10, 20 or 30 years as an expert in their field (Committee). These *adaptive experts* approach new situations with flexibility, and become lifelong learners. They are skilled at using not only what they have learned, but also in the concept of metacognition, so that they continually question their own expertise and attempt to move into ever higher levels of knowledge. (Ibid.)

While experts do have well-honed information retrieval systems, and are more likely to have answers to complex problems, they are not simply general problem solvers. They have well-defined strategies that enable them to operate across all domains. However, the key to their expertise over others is their capacity to recognize meaningful patterns of information in all domains, not just in their field of expertise (ibid). By seeing patterns of meaningful information early in the problem-solving process, experts can begin problem-solving at "a higher place" (De Groot). Pattern recognition also provides them with "triggers" for learning, storing, and accessing relevant knowledge for more complex problems.

Experts are quick to think in terms of core concepts and big ideas, while the novice is far more likely to seek correct formulas and pat answers based on their intuition to solve problems.

In the development of experts, teachers and mentors must develop curricula and learning opportunities that emphasize depth of knowledge over breadth. As teachers and mentors it is important to share with mentees models of how experts organize and solve problems, so they too can understand the process.

Obviously, experts possess a vast repertoire of knowledge, yet only a small subset is relevant to any specific problem (Committee). Rather than conducting an exhaustive search of everything they know, experts rely on retrieval of information relevant to the task at hand. In order to be retrieved quickly, knowledge must be "conditionalized" in order to be properly filed and retrieved when needed.

Simply providing "facts and formulas" without assisting mentees in developing the learning conditions under which the knowledge may be used through knowledge conditioning, is a disservice to mentees.

"In the development of experts [out of mentees], teachers and mentors must develop curricula and learning opportunities that emphasize depth of knowledge over breadth."

Mentees must also be taught how to retrieve relevant information and knowledge in an "effortless" manner. Doing so enables mentees to place fewer demands on conscious attention, which is a limited human capacity. It is far better to place emphasis on a learner's capacity to understand complex problems and their subcomponents rather than requiring the learner to focus on perfectly remembering facts instead of learning.

An important point for all to remember is that expertise in an area does not guarantee that one can effectively teach others about that area. To make new information meaningful, expert teachers and mentors must also understand the difficulties students face in tapping into the mentor's existing knowledge.

[E]xpertise in an area does not guarantee that one can effectively teach others about that area.

The true mark of an expert is in *knowing* the extent of one's knowledge, rather than assuming one knows everything, then moving forward to learn even more. This in turn, opens the mind to *lifelong learning*.

Characteristics of Experts

Over time, experts will develop several key principles to enhance their knowledge. The following are characteristics that mentors and mentees should continually strive to develop to refine their learning processes:

Information patterns. Experts, especially accomplished novices, develop the capacity for noticing features and meaningful patterns of information that are overlooked by others.

Organization of knowledge. Over time, experts acquire a great deal of content knowledge, which they organize to reflect a much deeper understanding of their subject matter, rather than memorizing specific words and phrases and problem approaches.

Integrated applicability. Experts develop integrated knowledge patterns that cannot be reduced to sets of isolated facts or propositions. Instead, their knowledge reflects "contexts of applicability." In arranging the information in this fashion, the experts knowledge is said to be "conditionalized" on a set of circumstances.

Easy retrieval of integrated information. With their knowledge integrated to an application, experts have the flexibility to retrieve important aspects of this knowledge base with little cognitive effort.

Flexibility. Not all experts are alike in this as different experts will have varying levels of flexibility in their approach to new, complex problem situations, but a flexible mindset is needed.

Information Patterns

Early researchers who studied how experts, particularly world-class chess masters who could consistently outthink their competitors, demonstrated how individual experts are. In their studies, the same stimulus was found to be understood differently, depending on the knowledge level of the expert in question at that particular time and as applied to the situation (De Groot).

In their research they found that, while both chess masters and lesser ranked players considered the breadth and depth of thinking in determining possible next moves, neither the masters nor the other players were able to consider all possible moves. (Figure 5.1.) But the chess masters were able to consider possible moves of much higher quality than those by inexperienced players. Rather than their outstanding memory recall of all possible moves, the experts relied upon their thousands of hours of chess playing—and the subsequent knowledge acquired—to recognize meaningful configurations and the associated strategic implications of a particular situation.

Figure 5.1. Strategy requires cognitive thinking

Source: Dejan Jovanovic/stock.adobe.com

These chess masters were able to assimilate a readily apparent, meaningful pattern that others could not, leading the researchers to this interesting conclusion:

> We know that increasing experience and knowledge in a specific field (chess, for instance) has the effect that things (properties, etc.) which, at earlier stages, had to be abstracted, or even inferred are apt to be immediately perceived at later stages. To a rather large extent, abstraction is replaced by perception, but we did not know much about how this works, nor where the borderline lies. As an effect of this replacement, a so-called "given" problem situation is not really given since it is seen differently by an expert than is perceived by an inexperienced person (ibid).

The experts' superior recall ability is based upon their capacity to group various elements of information related to buy an underlying strategy. Since our short-term memory is limited,

learners can enhance their memory by clustering information
into familiar patterns. However, novices must have a deeper
background in the area to develop the structure necessary to
encode these meaningful chunks of information. This research
provided a foundation for specialized learning that has been
cross validated through the use of other learning methodologies
(Erickson; Ericsson).

Since our short-term memory is limited,
learners can enhance their memory by clustering information into familiar patterns.

Experience in a particular domain provides the foundation
for development of sensitivity to patterns within the domain and
the ability to arrange information in a meaningful way. Clustering of information based upon previous depth of the subject
has been demonstrated for experts in a wide variety of domains,
including electronic circuitry, radiology, and computer programming. In each of these areas more experienced individuals were
able to reproduce large portions of complex diagrams, such as
circuit diagrams, after only a few seconds of viewing. These
experts were able to group several individual circuit elements,
for example the amplifier circuit elements, and then re-create the
diagram by remembering the structure and function of a typical
amplifier rather than memorizing each of the elements or components of the diagram (Committee).

In teaching, both the teacher and mentor can improve their
students' pattern recognition by providing learning experiences
that specifically enhance their ability to recognize meaningful
patterns of information within a particular field, rather than
memorizing individual components.

It is important to share with mentees how the mentor conceptualizes ideas within their field of expertise.

Organizational Knowledge

An expert's mind is organized around core concepts, or "big ideas" that guide their thinking in their field of expertise (ibid). These big ideas are generally considered major principles or laws applicable to a particular field of study. Rather than approaching the problem by focusing on specific equations that could be used and manipulated to solve a problem, an expert will first organize the problem around the big ideas to understand how to formulate a general approach to the problem.

Consider an example from physics. When given a complex physics problem, an expert will identify the major principles and laws, such as the laws of thermodynamics that guide their strategic thinking about the problem, whereas a novice rarely refers to a problem by its major principles. Instead, novices react by remembering specific equations and identifying how they would manipulate those equations to solve the problem.

From this example, we can see how learning will enhance or hinder our ability to organize information around a particular subject. By merely memorizing, recalling and manipulating equations, students are limiting their capacity to understand the broader, more complex problems. Evolution into an expert in a particular area requires understanding of the broader principles involved, as well as the specific memorization of equations associated with that principle and, more importantly, development of a framework of organization for facts about the problem that goes beyond the mere surface characteristics.

To better understand this concept, consider solving the following question to understand how adults and children react to this problem:

A father and his two children are standing on a bridge looking down into the river. The daughter is able to count five turtles sunning themselves on the nearest shoreline, while the son, looking directly down into the water, saw two very large fish below the bridge. If the father is six feet tall, how high is the bridge above the water?

Adults can quickly recognize the information provided in the question is not related to the question being asked, it is therefore irrelevant, and the problem unsolvable. Children, however, will often begin formulating how they can add, subtract, divide or otherwise manipulate the numerical information provided to solve the problem.

While this is a very simple, and perhaps silly example it illustrates the difference between mere memorization of equations applied to solve a problem, rather than a more complex understanding of the question at hand.

An expert's capacity for organizing knowledge therefore requires an in-depth coverage of topics, as well as assistance from teachers and mentors concerning ideas on how students can organize information for rapid recall.

Integrated Applicability

While experts have a vast repertoire of knowledge relevant to their discipline, only a subset of that knowledge may be relevant to a specific problem (Committee). The key to expert problem-solving is not in the expert's capacity to recall every detail that may be pertinent to a problem, as that would quickly overload the brain's memory circuits. The issue then becomes how to quickly retrieve knowledge specific and relevant to a particular task.

Cognitive scientists referred to this as *conditionalized knowledge*, since the information includes a specification of the context in which it is useful (Simon "On the Development"; Glaser). We refer to this concept as *integrated applicability*, or how the mind can organize and integrate the information to a useful application or context.

In learning, students usually encounter textbooks and teachers who can abundantly explain laws and theories, but rarely discuss how these laws may be useful in solving problems (Simon). Over time students may or may not integrate their information to applications. In many cases the information remains "inert," that is, the information has been stored in memory but cannot be called upon to help solve problems since it is not tied to any direct application. It becomes just another random fact.

Teachers and mentors can assist students in developing integrated applicability of information by presenting word problems requiring students to use appropriate concepts and formulas (Simon "Problem Solving"; Lesgold "Acquring Expertise," "Problem Solving"). These word problems can be designed to help students learn when, where, and why the information is important and how it can be applied.

EASY RETRIEVAL OF INTEGRATED INFORMATION

With their knowledge integrated to an application, experts have the flexibility to retrieve important aspects of their knowledge base with little cognitive effort. This capacity to transfer knowledge is affected by the degree to which people learn with understanding rather than merely memorize facts (Committee).

To learn with understanding takes time. Researchers estimate that world-class chess masters require approximately 50,000 to 200,000 hours of practice to reach their level of expertise. At the same time their knowledge base will rely on 50,000 familiar chess patterns that guide selection of moves (Chase). This information is not gained overnight. Much time is involved in the development of these pattern recognition skills, which in turn will provide the expert with a fluent identification of meaningful patterns, as well as their knowledge of the implications for future outcomes.

Understanding is the key to easy retrieval and transfer of integrated information. Students must be encouraged to see the relationships in a given field rather than memorizing information by rote. While students who have learned tasks by rote memorization can perform the same or similar tasks based on memorization of a solution formula, they are unable to transfer the information to novel problems and applications (Committee).

At this point it might be worthwhile to note that even the most talented students require a great deal of practice and task commitment and dedication in order to develop their expertise (Ericsson). At first, students may need considerable time to explore underlying concepts and generate connections to other information they have learned. If the teacher or mentor covers many topics too quickly, this may actually hinder learning and subsequent transfer of information, as students will learn only isolated sets of facts without having the organization or connection necessary for rapid recall. If students are introduced to organizing principles early, this may also hinder their learning as they will not be able to retain specific knowledge to make the relationships meaningful (ibid). Research is shown that by providing students opportunities to encounter specific, relevant information on a topic early, provides a better learning outcomes from an organizing lecture (ibid).

In addition to grappling with subjects, students must also have enough time to learn to process the information. Once again learning cannot be rushed as the complex cognitive activity of information integration and transfer requires time (Committee). Of course, there are also variables which affect our learning in the amount of time necessary to master a particular field. Some factors influencing transfer include; context, motivation to learn, problem representations, relationships between learning and transfer conditions, as well as active and passive approaches to transfer. Which learning method is most effective depends upon the individual, however those students

Sidebar 5.1. The road less traveled makes the difference

MADHUSOODAN HOSUR, HEAD
Protein Crystallography Section, Bhabha Atomic Research Centre, Mumbai, India

Going into a doctorate program at the Indian Institute of Science, I was ranked No. 2 in the admission merit list, so I could pretty much choose a PhD advisor from among the university's faculty. One professor, Prof. Viswamitra, despite being a full-fledged professor with a great international reputation, was known to be simple and approachable by students. So, when it was my turn to pick a guide, simplicity was the word that made me join, without batting an eyelid, Prof. Viswamitra as his PhD student.

Prof. Viswamitra practiced what he preached; "Hosur, we should research new things," he suggested several times. He was the only professor to pursue research in biology in the Department of Physics! While most scientists chose proteins as their research objects, Prof. Viswamitra chose to be different by selecting for research the less studied and challenging nucleic acid molecules.

Following his advice, after finishing my PhD I chose to work on a hugely challenging research problem: the structures of icosahedral viruses—molecules a million times smaller than viruses. But the rewards have been very satisfying because I was the first person in the world to determine the three dimensional structures of an insect virus.

Successful mentors censure mentees for their wrong doings without alienating them. I still remember the way Prof. Viswamitra handled the situation when I had let an X-ray generator run without ensuring a supply of water to cool the anode. He displayed a quality in successful mentors I have observed: The art of making the communication a two-way process. This means eliciting from mentees their thoughts about mistakes and what could have avoided it; and letting mentees realize for themselves the errors and correct paths in the future; rather than a mentor pointing out mistakes and explaining correct processes. This brings into mentees a feeling of ownership which eggs mentees to do their best.

While guiding trainees or graduate students I have tried to inculcate the above factors into my mentoring. And I advise students to be curious and interested in things around them, to be articulate within limits, to strive for perfection at every stage, and to believe in themselves. I tell my students: "Do any job not to please others but yourself." This, I find, instills motivation, which is everything for success in any walk of life.

engaged in "deliberate practice" including active monitoring of the learning experience appear to master their areas most effectively (ibid).

Sidebar 5.1 on page 103 illustrates the challenges students face with unfamiliar or unchartered territory. Despite the greater risks and efforts, this is where discoveries are to be found, rather than covering known ground that has already been studied. And such ventures are bound to result in mistakes and failures, but they are the roads to discovery and learning.

CONTEXT OF ORIGINAL LEARNING

The context of original learning is a very important variable in the information transfer process. Context refers to the environment and situation surrounding the original learning experience. For example, a child may have difficulty originally learning mathematics in the classroom setting, but when surrounded by a woodworking shop and an opportunity to conduct hands-on carpentry mathematics and fractions in particular may be much easier for the individual to grasp. Place them back in the school environment and they will be unable to pass the exams. How tightly learning is tied to context depends upon how the knowledge is acquired (Eich).

For transfer to be effective the subject must be taught in multiple contexts rather than in a single context. An effective technique to do this is to have learners elaborate on examples they have used during learning to facilitate retrieval at a later time. A note of caution here, however. This activity of reinforcing to a particular transfer item may actually make it more difficult to retrieve the lesson material in other contexts, as knowledge also tends to be "context bound" when learners tie a particular context to only one contextual situation.

This can be overcome by teachers and mentors providing additional context and principles to which information can be attached.

Motivation

The key element with motivation is the amount of time students are willing to devote to learning. A motivated student will develop competency more quickly than a disinterested student. While extrinsic rewards and punishments clearly affect behavior, a student's intrinsic motivation may allow the motivated student to exceed the learning of those strictly receiving extrinsic rewards or punishments.

For effective motivation, challenges must be at the proper level of difficulty to remain motivating. If tasks are too easy, students may perceive the learning experience to be boring, while tasks that are too difficult can cause frustration and significant loss of motivation. Another concept that comes into play in this regard is the students orientation towards "performance" or "learning" (Dweck). Learning oriented students anticipate and thrive on new challenges, while those who are performance oriented are much more concerned about making errors than about learning. Failure is an option! Students must embrace the opportunity to fail as a learning experience, not as a punishment or an activity that results in complete lack of self-esteem. It is critical for the teacher and mentor to understand their students and to adjust to the proper level of a challenge in order to continue motivating their students.

Several other factors affect motivation, including a student's sense of contributing to others. Sharing in a social environment is an important concept, where many students quickly rise to an opportunity to exchange information and ideas with other students. This includes writing stories, presenting artwork and other activities.

Other learners may be motivated when they can see the usefulness of what they are learning and are able to use that information to impact others. This is an especially important concept for local community and environmental concerns. Projects with strong social consequences such as tutoring others, were making presentations to outside audiences can motivate students by giving them a sense of pride, success, and creativity (McCombs; Pintrich).

Problem Representation

By instructing students to represent problems at higher levels of abstraction, teachers and mentors will be able to create a greater opportunity for knowledge transfer (Committee).

Flexibility

Not all experts are alike, as different experts will have varying levels of flexibility in their approach to new, complex problem situations (ibid).

EFFECTIVE TEACHING

While learning theory may not provide simple basic recipes for designing effective learning environments, new developments in the science of learning raise important questions for teachers and mentors on how to design better learning environments (Committee). Teachers and mentors demand much more of their students today than was expected 100 years ago. By the same token students demand more of their teachers and mentors. Different learning goals require different approaches to instruction, which in turn will lead to changes and opportunities to learn. Four perspectives are particularly important based upon current research in human learning in providing opportunities to design quality learning environments.

Today, students must be adept at understanding the current state of their knowledge and building upon it, improving it, and making decisions in the face of uncertainty unlike students of the past who could get by using rote memorization, or emulation sufficient to pass an exam on specific memorized topics and subsequent details (Talbert). Today's graduates must be able to identify and solve problems and make complex contributions to society. To do so, the students must have the skills necessary for adaptive expertise. Teachers and mentors must rethink what and how topics are taught, and more importantly how students learn and are assessed.

While best introduced and explained as individual perspectives, the four perspectives on learning environments important to today's students and learning are actually mutually supportive, and must be considered as a system of interconnected components.

Learner-Centered

"Learner-centered" refers to environments that pay careful attention to the knowledge, skills, attitudes, and beliefs that learners bring to the educational setting (Committee). This perspective also incorporates culturally relevant, appropriate and responsive teaching practices. Learning-centered teaching cultivates students thinking in relation to the problems at hand in order to understand and discuss student misperceptions, and provides them learning situations in which to readjust their ideas (Bell "Diagnosing").

Starting with the structure of a child's knowledge, teachers and mentors can formulate a basis to diagnose knowledge that has already been acquired through observation, questioning and conversation as well as a reflection on the student's activities. Teachers and mentors can facilitate their understanding of this information by prompting children to explain and develop their knowledge structures. This can be achieved by asking them to make predictions about various situations and explain the reasons for their predictions. If teachers and mentors are aware of common misperceptions, they can help students test their thinking and see how and why various ideas held by the students might need to be modified in some way (Bell "Treating").

Teachers and mentors must be culturally attuned to their students, deliberately learning about their home and community cultural practices, as well as languages used, and incorporating these into mentoring to reinforce learning opportunities. This includes identifying the students' common, or colloquial language, explaining concepts in their common language, then gradually moving the student into an understanding of the objective, expository thought process and communication style most common within academic circles.

Teachers and mentors facilitating learner-centered environments are aware learners construct their own meanings around their beliefs, understandings and cultural practices as reference points. Teachers must understand what their students know and can do, as well as their interests and passions in order to build upon these to achieve greater motivation and meet learning goals as the teachers and mentors stretch their young minds to build new understandings.

Knowledge Centered

The ability of experts to think and solve problems, as we have seen, requires not just a generic set of thinking skills or learning strategies, but is founded upon a base of well-organized knowledge that support planning and strategic thinking. Teachers and mentors facilitating a knowledge centered environment understand the need to help students become more knowledgeable by learning deeply but not superficially. This requires understanding and subsequent transfer of knowledge. Knowledge-centered and learner-centered environments intersect, as students' initial preconceptions on the subject matter are carefully considered so that the learning environment can focus on background information that is essential to a comprehensive understanding of new information.

Integral to knowledge-centered learning environments is an emphasis on "sense making" or, helping students use metacognitive thinking. For example, in mathematics students are quite often taught the process of calculation or computation involving only application of a set formula with no consideration for ingenuity or flair, nor an opportunity for discovery. While learning to "compute" is an essential part of mathematics, students must also be exposed to "thinking" which can only occur when they are able to understand and make sense of the mathematics by using underlying principles and connections of all of the mathematical components.

One way to achieve this is through the approach of "progressive formalization." Beginning with the ideas the students bring to school, teachers and mentors can gradually help their students to see how these ideas can be transformed and formalized. Each instructional unit encourages students to build on in formal ideas in a gradual but structured manner in order to acquire the concepts and procedures of the discipline (Committee).

THE MENTORING MINDSET

Each of us has the capacity for mentoring others, whether from a natural gift of interacting with people, or from working to develop our interactive skills. One of the most critical characteristics is development of the mentoring mindset which begins with our capacity to keep growing as a person and as a leader.

The mentoring mindset requires that we begin thinking like a mentor. We need to be able to make development of other people our top priority. In mentoring, unlike teaching in an educational classroom, we work with only one mentee at a time, rather than a group. Our mentees must be specially selected and adapted for the journey. Before we can begin this journey of course, we will have to develop relationships through understanding of our selected mentees. As we begin the journey we must also develop our capacity to give help unconditionally, cultivating a "win-win" relationship. Throughout the journey, our mentees must become engaged with us in the activities that we perform, so that they too can experience what we are experiencing, and so that we can impart knowledge through this "on the job training." We must also provide resources for our mentees, by sharing books, podcasts, videos, and our experiences with the people that we are developing.

The mentoring mindset also requires cultivation of the flight instructor's capacity to impart knowledge, subdue fear, and ultimately let our mentees take a solo flight free from our supervision. It's very difficult for the mentor to actually let go by providing clear direction for the solo flight, clearing obstacles in the mentee's pathway, then patting them on the back and turning them loose to succeed. Of course, the mentor must always be there to congratulate them on their success, pick them up, dust them off from their failure, and send them back into the air.

A final element of the mentoring mindset requires the mentor to prepare the mentee to pick up the mantle as a mentor for the next generation, constantly lifting each succeeding generation to a higher plateau. A great mentoring relationship will naturally give way to a subsequent great mentoring career if the protégé has witnessed great mentoring first hand.

■ ■ ■

KEY POINTS ABOUT THE MENTORING MINDSET

In this chapter we considered various ways to convert information into knowledge and methods for transfering knowledge to others. Following are key points to remember about learning and the mind:

1. Focusing on how people learn helps mentors move beyond the basics of the lecture and evaluation approach of traditional education, and helps students understand and develop basic skills for thinking and problem-solving.

2. The student's preconceptions and levels of understanding must be determined to monitor their learning outcome. There is no universal "best" teaching practice.

3. When solving problems, experts usually begin with trying to understand the problem rather than immediately inserting numbers or reaching for undeveloped solutions. On the other hand, a novice tends to reach a solution without fully comprehending the problem.

4. Experts have well-honed mental information retrieval systems and well-defined strategies for problem-solving, however their real expertise lies in recognizing patterns of meaningful information early in the problem-solving process. This is what mentors should seek to develop in their protégés.

5. Area expertise does not guarantee effectiveness in teaching others about that area.

6. Experts develop over time by developing information patterns, ways to organize knowledge, integrated applicable and he of knowledge, easy retrieval of integrated information, and flexibility in problem solving.

CHAPTER

6

Mentoring to Build Character

To educate a man in mind and not in morals
is to educate a menace to society.

—Theodore Roosevelt

E DUCATORS, PARENTS, MENTORS and others strive to create and support structured programs, opportunities and lessons to engage students in a variety of activities, including academics, sports, and community service. Why?

Within their lives each of them found within these types of programs opportunities for learning, variously described as character education, positive youth development, social and emotional learning, interpersonal and intrapersonal competencies, or noncognitive skills. While these terms are not interchangeable, there is overlap among them. These skills and attributes provide the foundation for our interactions in the workplace and in our personal lives by allowing us to manage our emotions, set and achieve positive goals, feel and show empathy, maintain positive relationships, and overall make sound decisions. Combined, these skills, traits, and characteristics can be referred to as *character*.

We use the word 'character' with wide applications every day in our language. While many people do not agree with a specific, shared definition of character, nor whether character can be a subject of research, analyzed to develop appropriate building blocks and taught, nearly everyone agrees that character is necessary and essential in today's complex world.

We recognize and respond positively to people who are responsible, honorable, and emotionally healthy—all essential characteristics of character. But character is a complex trait requiring various experiences with which to shape the final outcome. Character is "not fixed by genes," but rather an outcome of a person's context and experiences. Leading the way is a synthesis of moral reasoning (Beatty). Perhaps character can best be understood as "a multifaceted developmental system rather than a set of traits" within an individual (Nucci).

Traditionally we think of character as consisting of honesty, fairness, and compassion—all of which must be defined within a particular cultural context, and worthy of developing as traits in our youth. These traditional traits are often considered "virtues" and associated with religious or philosophical traditions more than a general framework for social interaction. Previous attempts at defining have consisted of only identifying a "bag of virtues"(Kohlberg) of which there may be a near infinite list of key virtues with very little overlap (Lapsley).

Amaresh Chakrabarti gives us one example of the importance and effects of such virtues on mentees and others, as shown in Sidebar 6.1 on page 115. Our point here is that mentors are influential because of exemplary behavior and virtues, as well as expertise. Their extraordinary "lessons," intended or not, can

Sidebar 6.1. A magnanimous word is greater than the insult

AMARESH CHAKRABARTI, SENIOR PROFESSOR & CHAIR
Department of Design and Manufacture, Indian Institute of Science, Bengaluru

Rajiv Krishnan, a fellow Pakistani and batch-mate (same graduating year) at Cambridge University, England, was my mentor in compassion and its power in human transformation.

On a Friday night in Cambridge, Rajiv and I were returning from a dinner. As we walked past a young, Caucasian couple, the man shouted at us, "Dirty Pakis, go back to your own country!"

Instead of getting scared or angry, Rajiv calmly went to the man and asked, "I would be happy to go back, but you must tell me why you are angry with us!"

Embarrassed, the lady tried to take the man away, but Rajiv was insistent with the man that it be discussed right away! In a few minutes the two were in deep conversation, as the lady and I stood by silently, surprised at the transformation. As we were to leave, the man apologized to Rajiv with a sincerity and fondness shown only to friends long known.

remain with us long after. In this example Rajiv, a Pakistani doctoral student in England, converted an insulting bigot into an understanding friend through gentle, rational persuasion, to the amazement of Rajiv's friend and the antagonist's companion.

The John Templeton Foundation, a leading organization in funding character-related work, seeks projects that promote an interesting set of qualities including; "all, creativity, curiosity, diligence, entrepreneurialism, forgiveness, future mindedness, generosity, gratitude, honesty, humility, joy, love, purpose, reliability, and thrift." One of the widely held concepts upon which character is based, regardless of cultural context, identify stages of individual growth in their capacity for moral judgment. This moral judgment is based upon the principles of justice and fairness, as well as the welfare of others, placing "morality" at the center of any meaningful notion of character (Kohlberg).

Recent research in character has raised such topics as, "grit," "social intelligence" and "emotional intelligence" as key character attributes. However, important as these traits are in the pursuit of personal and social benefits, they can be applied for either positive or negative goals, not leading directly to moral or immoral actions, and therefore are "not a sufficient indicator of a person's character" (Kohlberg). Indeed, many researchers in the field of moral education have abandoned the term "character," preferring the terms "moral self" or "moral identity" (Nucci; Kohlberg).

Mentors can best define and clarify character for their mentees only if they too, have a clear idea of what it is and what it is not. The most useful focus for character development may be in terms of the concept of "moral agency" (ibid). Moral agency is the capacity to base one's actions on goals and beliefs concerning morality, which begins in childhood. As children grow and interact in their social networks, children begin to make sense of the consequences of their own and others' actions. Moral agency is just one element in this complex system of self—growing, expanding and constantly evolving as we go through life.

Character then, is an unfinished product, which is continuously evolving. It is also interactive.

Character by its very nature consists of interactions between an individual and the environment, including the choices and actions an individual takes. We demonstrate character by behaving in a rational manner across varied situations, rather than consistently displaying a single trait or set of traits (ibid).

Nucci identified four critical components of what can be considered the "Character System." These four elements include:

• Moral cognition

• Emotional development for moral mental health

• Performance

• Moral (critical) social engagement

We can examine these in more detail in the following pages.

Moral Cognition

Moral cognition refers to a "willful decision to act morally" (Nucci). Each day we are faced with moral decisions that may require only a little deliberation, or other decisions requiring a great deal of contemplation with multiple, competing considerations. Whether easy or difficult, these decisions can be grouped into three general categories. The first, "moral judgments" refers to our struggles to make decisions based upon the welfare of others, fairness, or rights. The second group are those decisions we make concerning actions within social conventions that is to say within the norms established by consensus or authority within a particular social group. Finally, we must also make decisions based upon factors related to our own personal choice and privacy.

While there are not yet defined stages of development in people's capacity to coordinate competing considerations within our complex social networks, moral judgments are tied to the specific context within which the assessment is made. This context is based upon the maturity and experience, as well as preconceived notions and information of the person making the moral judgment.

The role of the mentor and teacher in this environment is to help the individual understand the basis upon which individuals are making moral judgments and to think deeply about that context, so the individual truly understands the basis for their moral judgments. Keep in mind, the mentor's goal here is to allow the mentee to illuminate and understand their judgments, not to change foundational beliefs. Once the mentee understands foundational aspects of how and why they are making these moral judgments, they will then have the tools to either reinforce those beliefs or change them.

Emotional Development, or "Moral Mental Health"

Moral mental health refers to the capacity of using empathy, and a sense of moral agency, as well as the ability to accurately read others' emotions in order to make judgments about what harm might come to others. These capacities might be negatively or positively enhanced by exposure to a variety of conditions in childhood (Beatty; Nucci).

Research suggests that current educational programs designed to enhance a child's capacity for social and emotional learning and to regulate their own behavior can also be used to optimize an individual's moral mental health (ibid). These programs are currently used by educators to overcome early childhood exposure to negative conditions which have created severe deficiencies in the child's moral mental health.

Social and emotional learning are elements of this moral component, as they are essential to moral functioning. However, these elements do not in themselves lead to more behaviors (ibid).

Moral Performance

Moral Performance is capacity of character enabling individuals to recognize the right thing to do, and to act on that judgment. The key element in understanding moral performance is that in taking action to do the right thing, the performance may come at a cost. Escalating costs of action may become so high that in certain situations, individuals may rationalize and "prioritize self-interests over the morally right thing to do" (ibid). Consider the case of child soldiers who are ordered to take immoral actions, or face dire consequences, perhaps including their own deaths for refusing to obey the orders of their superiors.

Acting on moral judgments then, may be more than simply demonstrating willpower or individual motivation. Being able to act on moral judgments in order to behave "morally" will compete with other internal goals and require a capacity for self-regulation and the ability to control one's own behavior.

The concept of "grit," defined as the capacity to both feel passion for a long-term goal and persevere in pursuing it (Duckworth), may be an important element of moral performance (Nucci). Researchers are investigating whether grit, "might help to explain the individual's commitment to addressing injustices despite extreme challenges" (Beatty; Nucci). While this may explain why moral actions are taken, it does not account for the moral thinking leading up to the decision to act (ibid).

Moral Social Engagement

Moral cognition, moral mental health, and moral performance characteristics that describe the development of an individual who will most likely "operate morally in everyday life." (Ibid). But, how then can one address the cognitive dissonance in the reality of our social structures and cultures? For example, how is it possible that people can live within a culture or society that is structurally unequal or incorporate such practices as slavery that an individual within the society may consider as being immoral?

The concept of moral social engagement is the capacity to take a critical moral stance, recognizing both that one's own moral perspective "may be faulty and that societal norms may be at odds with fairness and respect for human welfare" (Nucci). Each individual in the society plays a role and has individual position within the larger social network. The capacity to contribute to "principled moral change" in the social system or "civic virtue" is another element of character (ibid). As an individual matures and becomes part of the social network surrounding them they also tend to develop personal goals they give an individual life meaning and direction, and often in terms of pursuit of social justice.

Character then, cannot be considered a collection of virtues or traits (Nucci). Character is a system that enables the person to engage the social world morally. While we may consider the individual components of it, character itself remains more than the sum of its parts. Character must be viewed and assessed by assessing the components of the character system, which are social and emotional learning, moral reasoning, and moral mental health.

CAN CHARACTER BE BUILT?

If one were to seek a course in character, they would quickly become disenchanted, as there is no one size, nor shape, nor even agreed upon curricula to develop character. Most certainly the individual components of character can be analyzed, assessed and taught.

The VIA Institute on Character is a nonprofit organization conducting research into and identifying ways to develop a comprehensive picture of character. In their model, they identify six universal virtues and strengths (Beatty) that can be found in everyone in one degree or another. From these virtues, it may be possible to help us develop the underlying principles essential in building character.

However, within these virtues, three factors may be most appropriate in teaching character. These factors are caring, inquisitiveness, and self-control. These three factors form what some researchers consider the three essential strengths or universal virtues for character. These three strengths enable teachers and mentors to teach their mentees to be "caring without the expectation of benefit, to be questioning without a crisis, and to be disciplined without structure" (McGrath).

As we begin mentoring our students we must constantly recognize that people have personal, interpersonal and cultural values that together contribute to a life well lived" (ibid).

CHARACTER AND CONTEXT

To understand any developmental phenomenon, such as character, it's important to recognize the reciprocal influences individuals have on one another (Beatty). Character development cannot be reduced to any one, single element. Rather, the character development system must be viewed in a holistic perspective.

Character is contextually defined (Beatty), representing a function of continuous mutually reinforcing relationships between the individual, the environment and the contextual area in which character is displayed. Character is displayed across time and place as a coherent strand of the individual's behavior, asserting itself with "the right virtue, in the right amount, at the right time" (Aristotle).

In examining individual pathways to development, mentors and teachers must be able to assess not just the differences between people as is commonly measured in the social sciences, but changes within the individual in the areas being taught or nurtured. This "person-centered analysis" is critical to the assessment and future growth of mentees. This area of research is beginning to blossom and many new tools are being developed for use by both the mentee, as well as teachers and teachers.

CHARACTER AND CULTURE

Cultural context is another crucial element influencing character development. Much like defining "character," "culture" is another concept that we all understand but may not be able to define. In the 1950s, anthropologist Alfred Kroeber and Clyde Kluckoholn identified more than 152 definitions of the term "culture" (Suárez). From the definitions and characteristics identified, they subsequently synthesized five essential elements of culture: values, beliefs, rituals, symbols, and practices. Each of these is expressed daily as a part of our character.

Mentors and teachers must strive to identify opportunities for young people to practice in a real-world context how to become men and women of character. This includes making judgments about what is right and wrong, and making decisions with courage and conviction concerning how to pursue concrete goals.

So, what are the practical challenges of developing character and what works most effectively in developing character?

APPROACHES TO BUILDING CHARACTER

Character education is "a way of being," fostered by educators, mentors, parents, other adults and role models, according to Marvin Berkowitz of the University of Missouri in St. Louis. As a preeminent researcher in the area of character development, Berkowitz established a structure for thinking about best practices in character education called PRIME, an acronym for "Prioritizing character education, Relationships, Intrinsic Motivation, Modeling, and Empowerment."

During Berkowitz' research, when people were asked about how their character traits were developed, most respond that they "worked to emulate a parent or other role model," or determined negative traits they saw in their parents and others around them and determined to correct these areas in their own life (ibid). Interestingly, people never seem to respond that their character was built through "the curriculum or set of lessons" (ibid).

Developmental psychologists and researchers would agree. Since people are complex organisms the idea that character can be "taught" does not fit within the model of human psychological or moral functioning used by psychology researchers. The goal of character development programs should therefore, not be to teach, "but to promote healthy adult cultures and actively foster young people's development" (ibid). In other words, character can't be taught, but it can be built!

Prioritizing Character Education

Prioritizing character education must be a genuine priority within the setting in which mentors and teachers are working to build character. Mentors should talk regularly about shared goals and values, communicating effectively to each other and to their mentees the importance of character development. This should be backed up with the appropriate resources and support within the programs to demonstrate that character education is a priority. This must be apparent to all from the top of the organization to the lowest levels. Everyone must incorporate character education as a key demonstrated value.

Relationships

Positive relationships at all levels must be cultivated by mentors and teachers, and consistently demonstrated to mentees. This includes cooperative learning opportunities for mentees, healthy competition as well as teaching interpersonal skills. Overall, respect must be demonstrated and cultivated in all interactions.

Intrinsic Motivation

Internalizing values and virtues is best done using strategies that engage students own motivations. By focusing on students' self-growth, and guiding them in setting goals, as well as offering focused training, mentors and teachers can instill an intrinsic motivation to their students. The most important aspect in the strategy however is allowing them opportunities to review their actions and behavior and begin initiating their own changes. These actions can be enhanced by offering opportunities to serve others and to engage in morally positive actions, and helping them to reflect on lessons they've learned.

Intrinsic motivation and the positive effects of empowerment

Sidebar 6.2. Different strokes for different folks

DR. HINA GOKHALE, DIRECTOR
Defense Metallurgical Research Laboratory (DMRL), India

In the early 1990s I was supervising a DMRL team at India's Defense Research and Development Organization (DRDO). We had developed several projects that we wanted to present to potential users. This team was staffed with bright, educated minds that excelled in researching ideas and producing presentations, but they were desk jockeys who were short on "persuasion"— getting out to the users in government and the defense community and explaining our concepts in terms they could digest. I knew we needed a different personality to round out the team, someone mobile and gregarious.

As I looked around the DRDO complex I noticed one person who I'll call "Pradesh" whom no group wanted because he was never at his desk. To the dismay of my team members and the surprise of others at the DRDO, I managed to convince the director to transfer Pradesh to my team.

To everyone's surprise and as I expected, Pradesh performed very well. The process of articulating projects and showing them became smooth and fast. Our new team member had his ways of dealing with files, people, and situations, but he was not compromising the lab's reputation, and he stayed within the rules and work got done. He bridged the gap between development and users.

People showed Pradesh their appreciation with special smiles.

He carved out a space for himself in the lab and his confidence level shot up. When I realized he didn't mind travelling on very short notice, I also put him in charge of our lab's exhibits, which needed to be sent to different locations far and near for various exhibitions.

He did well and our exhibits were always in place and appreciated by the visitors. As our "exhibitor," Pradesh became so self-driven that he made sure he familiarized himself with the projects so our intended audience would hear and see the exhibits, and appreciate their importance, in their terms.

In one particular event a three-ton "Titanium sponge cake"—a particularly important exhibit— was put up. The main leader for the project was scheduled to explain the technology to the then-Chief Minister (CM) of Andhra Pradesh, a state in India. Expecting the CM at a certain time, the project leader had gone to arrange for a bouquet of flowers for the event, but the CM arrived early and the project manager was absent. After some silence, and to not keep the CM waiting, Pradesh took charge of the situation, provided a captivating presentation, and got photographed for the media with the CM and the Titanium Sponge cake!

Pradesh has since retired but he continues to be self-driven and motivated. At 63 he qualified as a black belt kudo master and is a manager and coach of a national kudo team.

are illustrated by Hina Gokhale in Sidebar 6.2 on page 124. In this case, Pradesh was unwanted in an organization where he was the odd ball among engineering "geeks" but, in the right position and empowered, he became the self-driven missing piece that successfully bridged the star performers of a research laboratory to their audience of buyers.

Modeling

Modeling is probably the most powerful strategy in building character. It is essential for educators and mentors to provide role models upon which mentees core values, virtues and social, as well as emotional competencies can be built. Keep in mind that your mentees are viewing you both up close and from a distance. "What you do has more impact than what you say!" (Berkowitz.)

Empowerment

Students must be empowered to share in their education and character building. Mentors and teachers must be facilitators rather than directors in the educational process, which means letting go of authority to make certain decisions. In order to do so, teachers and mentors must assume some risk and, often reward behaviors which result in mistakes rather than issuing punishments, in order for the mentees to learn from their mistakes.

Empowerment to make decisions will also drive initiative to keep moving forward as the mentee learns, as Sidebar 6.2 on page 124 and Sidebar 6.3 on page 126 exemplify. The point of these anecdotes is that people can rise to the occasion when they are empowered and are given the opportunity and trust.

This does not mean that mistakes are overlooked, but rather the mistakes are identified and pointed out, as well as discussed. This provides a way to learn from our mistakes. How could a

Sidebar 6.3. The freedom to make and learn from mistakes

ELIZABETH GONZALEZ, FOUNDER AND CEO
Specialty HR Consulting, Miami, Florida, U.S.A.

Having just pivoted from a secure corporate job to entrepreneurship, I'm now looking at exciting new business challenges—and risks— to build my new startup. But I got the courage, skillsets, confidence, and guidance for this from mentors for whom I worked and who never expected anything in return.

It started when I was nineteen, working at a hotel as a front desk receptionist. When the supervisor position became available, the general manager said, "Liz, I see potential in you and you're the only one that completes the full shift reporting tasks every day. Apply and we'll see how it goes." This encouraged me despite knowing full well how young and inexperienced I was.

To my surprise, after the interviews of all internal and external candidates, I was chosen. This came with many challenges, as other more tenured employees had also applied and were not happy that they'd be managed by a *teenager*.

Soon after, the disgruntled front desk associates all stayed out one day to protest that the supervisor position had been granted to a less experienced and fairly new teammate. They believed their actions would lead me to give up and leave. But the hotel had to keep functioning, so I worked a straight 24-hour shift to keep operations flowing.

The general manager guided me through these challenges and supported me by providing managing tips, like setting clear expectations with the team, communicating effectively by listening actively, encouraging dialogue to address concerns, and leading by example.

It was difficult, but the experience made me stronger as an individual, and instilled responsibility and courage in me. It also prepared me for the coming years. I came to realize that despite hard times we need to move on anyway.

In my senior year of college, a professor had launched a behavioral health organization and advertised the office manager role to his students. I applied and was selected. This experience was, probably, the most pivotal moment of my entire working life so far. He entrusted me—a 20-something-year-old—with his business, and I took off, excited by this opportunity and eager to learn.

His mentoring strategy was simple: to give me the autonomy to "run," "learn" from my mistakes, and "push" me past limits I'd set for myself. My first task was to build out the billing department. I had no idea where to even begin, but I put my thinking hat on and started to do research. Through online resources and talks with insurance companies I gained an understanding of the diagnosis and billing codes system, among other things. As I navigated these uncomfortable new waters I leaned further into the fear of failure and made mistakes along the way, but I'd correct them, learn from them, and build a better process.

The freedom to make and learn from mistakes (continued)

Despite the many mistakes, I was never reprimanded. Instead, I was encouraged to "keep moving forward," a phrase the professor used often and I adopted.

Within a couple of years of being in business we grew from a tiny, shared office to the entire second floor of an office building. The business continued to grow and eventually sold for a very generous sum. This experience gave me the confidence I needed, and made me realize what I am capable of. I was unstoppable! ... until I wasn't.

An extreme catastrophe happened to my family. I lost my mother and I became the legal guardian to two young nieces. This shifted my path entirely. To cope with these new demands I took work with a large corporation that provided the stability, benefits, and time flexibility I needed to be my nieces' guardian.

Three particular mentors in that company helped me develop in the field of human resources, what I now specialize in. The first one, my boss, freed me to evolve and spread my wings while coaching me about "recruiting." Most importantly, whenever he could he'd mention my name to the senior leadership and gave me credit for the projects I had completed. He didn't care about himself; he cared about helping me grow.

I often called myself the black sheep of my family because I felt I was worlds apart from them. and he'd often remind me that I was "the *white* sheep of your family,

the one filled with hopes, dreams, and the work ethic to become anything you set my mind to." Those reminders were gold to me.

The second mentor was a leader in the HR department as well, but within the HR Business Partner area. His mentorship style was a bit different. He challenged me beyond my capabilities and forged me into a "diamond" with the pressure of his expectations.

Finally, the third mentor, the Chief People Officer, saw something within me that I failed to see: that I questioned my every decision or thought when working on projects. Copping with what had happened to my family, I had settled into a cocoon and lost all my confidence. He turned this around by challenging my thoughts to the breaking point. He'd challenge me to get away from a frail mindset and get back to who I truly was: outspoken and unstoppable.

Had I not been given the freedom to spread my wings, make mistakes, and learn, I wouldn't be the capable person I am today. My mentors' confidence in me let me grow, and their ability to see potential despite my own misgivings led me to understand that mistakes are part of the learning process. It changed my life, and it urges me to have the same impact in the lives of others. Their growth and accomplishments give me a sense of fulfillment.

We are not meant to go through life alone; "it takes a village," and I have firsthand experience in that it truly does.

task have been done better? In Sidebar 6.3 we see that one way is to allow—better yet, encourage—mentees to venture out and learn from mistakes.

An important component is also analyzing the risks taken in these decisions. Was it appropriate? Was it mitigated, and could it have been better mitigated? In this regard, it is important for students to understand the difference between standard operating procedures which have been established due to extensive experience, and perhaps mishaps that have led to "rules" that should in nearly all situations be applied, as opposed to operating techniques which may demonstrate a safe and efficient manner in which to accomplish a task, but which could be done differently with little or no increased risk.

Another important component of empowerment is the understanding of second and third order effects of decisions. Based upon the vast experience of educators and mentors, it is far easier for us to see the impacts and consequences of our current actions, whereas students with limited experience may be unable to understand all of the complex variables relating to and impacting future actions based upon current decisions. This is where the mentors can shine in identifying their experiences in way in which their mentees can glimpse some of those complex contexts upon which future outcomes are based. For understanding to occur, students must be challenged not only with action, but with opportunities for reflection.

TEACHING CHARACTER
AND SETTING HIGH EXPECTATIONS

Mentors and educators can approach the task of building character using two methodologies. The first is to explain and teach directly the elements and components of character building. While we mentioned earlier, character cannot be taught, but it can be explained. Directly discussing social and emotional competencies and helping mentees understand through our experiences provides one method of directly teaching character building.

Another method which goes hand-in-hand with direct teaching of character, is establishing high expectations for growth and clearly articulating these to our mentees. Integral to this approach is giving students the opportunity to practice the competencies they are learning. This can be done through real-world analysis, as well as role-playing, and most importantly teachers and educators setting the example as role models.

Ultimately, the role of mentors and educators is to not only to teach character building, but more to practice it ourselves in every aspect of our daily lives. It will also be up to our students to set their own standards and plan an active part in building their own character. As Aristotle once said, "We become just by the practice of just actions, self-controlled by exercising self-control, and courageous by performing acts of courage." (Larson). The more opportunities we can provide for our students to grapple with real-world challenges in a supportive environment with oversight and encouragement by trusted program leaders will be invaluable in preparing our youth for their future roles.

By challenging our mentees, we can cultivate a climate of character building as well as a culture of action, motivating our youth to both learn and to do. Integral to the success of these programs is the concept of respect, both given and received, as well as the concept of trust and empowerment. Our ultimate goal in character building is for our mentees to become people of character, rather than just acting good.

THE MEASURE OF CHARACTER

The importance of both implementing programs and evaluating their effectiveness has been demonstrated in many endeavors. This is no less the case in establishing effective programs to build character through mentorship. Implementation of programs is often far easier than measuring their outcomes, although Dr.

Joseph Durlak of Loyola University reminds us that, "unless you attend carefully to effective program implementation, you will probably be wasting valuable time, effort, and resources on new programs that are unlikely to be successful."

Research over the last 20 years has revealed that "the program you think you are doing almost never turns out to be the program that actually occurs" (ibid). Despite good intentions, programs often fail to overcome the realities encountered. There are four components of effective program implementation that will help in overcoming initial obstacles and in providing strong, flexible and adaptive programs.

Fidelity

Fidelity refers to the level at which major components of the program have been designed and delivered in the field.

Level of Delivery

When programs are initially conceived, the level of complexity can be very high. Upon implementation, facilitators may not be able to deliver all of the ingredients initially proposed in the program. Reduction of the dosage of the program, or how much of the program can be delivered, may significantly impact on the program's outcome. Program should be designed using the principle of simplicity whenever possible.

Quality of Delivery

Regardless of how well the program is designed, the true test of the program effectiveness will be in the quality of the program delivery. How well or competently the program is conducted and administered will be critical to achieving the stated program goals.

Adaptability

The great majority of programs will require changes to the original program. The best programs are those which anticipate adaptation, and allow room for scalability and growth while maintaining a clear path to their original goals and objectives. Program adaptations can and do make programs more effective, but it is imperative that a structured process be used to review potential changes, and clear lines of authority be drawn concerning those with the power to make decisions concerning adaptations. These decisions must be documented, and those affected by the decision must have "buy-in" to fully and effectively implement those decisions. Challenges do and will occur, requiring strong leadership and motivated staff in analyzing and refining new, or changed program goals, which can be accepted by all participants.

Perhaps the most important premise concerning program implementation and its effect on measurable outcomes is that extensive research has shown that when attention to the quality of implementation increases, outcomes improve (Durlak). Implementation can be affected by a wide variety of factors—more than twenty such factors have been identified in recent research (ibid). These factors range from the influence of the organization and its staff, as well as their involvement, to the community at large. Programs must be compatible with the setting and the populations they intend to serve. More importantly, the program leadership must be committed and have a shared vision of the outcomes the program intends to achieve.

There are three specific factors that have been shown to be important to effective overall program implementation. These include, professional development, possibilities for adapting the program or system, and effective leadership within the host organization. High quality professional development, including both training and ongoing support of those involved in the program is one of the most, if not the most important factor in achieving program success.

Those implementing new programs should be aware of barriers that new programs face, as well as environments that foster ineffective implementation. These barriers include competing priorities for both mentors and mentees; competing time and resources, as well as insufficient resources to complete the tasks required; and insufficient infrastructure. Of course, no list of barriers would be complete without the ever present "negative attitudes about the program," or "resistance to change" that may be encountered when dealing with everyone from the highest to the lowest levels. Quite simply, if any of these barriers are present and cannot be mitigated, the program is doomed to failure.

Effective leadership and clear allocation of responsibility and accountability, as well as flexibility within an organization are key elements in mitigating or eliminating barriers. All of these require effective communication to make the program productive.

SHOULD EVALUATION BE A LOW PRIORITY?

No program is ever planned, developed and implemented to fail. Yet many of them do. Why? Quite often planners and program implementers believe the results will speak for themselves, and therefore they provide little or no resources, nor thought on development of an effective evaluation program. Sufficient resources and time are simply not invested in evaluations, as almost everyone agrees that conducting activities within the program should receive the highest priority. After all, if the activities are not being completed, how can measurable outcomes be expected?

Measuring the effectiveness of a program requires a strong commitment to evaluation, as well as a trained and competent evaluation force. From development to program implementation, program evaluation must be on an equal footing with other priorities and cannot be overlooked. A judicious mix of quantitative and qualitative measures are critical in the evaluation process.

Measuring success requires expertise in conducting sound evaluations. Those evaluated programs, as well as the overall organization itself, must adopt an "evaluative thinking" approach (Trochim). This approach requires "critical thinking be applied in the context of evaluation, motivated by an attitude of inquisitiveness and belief in the value of evidence, that involves identifying assumptions, posing thoughtful questions, pursuing deeper understanding through reflection and perspective taking, and informing decisions in preparation for action" (Buckley).

Programs in character building should be thought of as "systems." After all, our definition of character demonstrated the interaction of multiple variables in a variety of key characteristics and elements. No single element can be isolated and evaluated, as our objective is to evaluate character "as a whole."

REINFORCING CHARACTER IN THE TWENTY-FIRST CENTURY

Character is a multidimensional concept, not easily separated into teachable or measurable components. The idea of character is, however, a tangible, necessary component of our mentoring in the 21st century. How well we do in preparing the future generations depends upon the efforts we exert now. Considerable research is underway in a variety of the components of character, as well as social and emotional learning. Within the next few years we may see an entire new field dedicated to research and development in character.

Organizations embarking on character building programs need to define for themselves, collaboratively which character goals the organization will pursue. The goal is to identify components of an individual program best suited to address character building from the standpoint of the implementing organization. The focus should be on behavior, making it clear to the individuals involved that within the context and culture identified there are specific "character components" being emphasized and developed, although "character" will be more than the sum of its elements.

By challenging our mentees, we can cultivate a climate of character building ...

Character building must also take into account the issues of race, income, class, gender, and culture. Each of these are key variables in the development and sustainability of character. Both mentors and mentees must be aware of the subconscious perceptions we have concerning each of these areas, and how these may color our character growth.

In mentoring students and preparing them for the 21st century, some basic structures are critically important to our efforts. Programs must have responsive engagement, and focus on development of reflection and critical thinking. In addition the programs must provide awareness and affirmation of the role of character building, and the mentee's role and motivation to inculcate positive character attributes in themselves and in assisting others. Character building, as in mentoring itself, is all about relationships. The stronger the relationship the more opportunity for gratifying results.

Character building cannot be done by simply modeling behaviors. Reflection on our behaviors and actions may be more important than the actions themselves, forcing us to understand and move our behaviors in a positive direction.

Professional development for those involved in character

building is a critical component, yet many programs do not have the resources, nor intentions to provide. In order to be able to mentor at the higher levels and, build character at ever higher levels requires advancement in the techniques and knowledge base for the mentors.

As in any professional program training and feedback is a key element. In order to improve, individuals must be critiqued in a positive but substantial manner on their actions and behaviors. Empowerment to take risks and make decisions is a critical component allowing mentees to forge their own path and learn from their lessons. The mentor must provide guidance and help mitigate the risk, but like pushing a young bird from the nest, the mentor must know and understand the mentee's capabilities and the timing of when to push them forward to fly.

Evaluation is another critical component. We must evaluate our programs and ensure that we are measuring the appropriate criteria that will drive overall results. This evaluation can be done through a variety of methods. Keep in mind that even the evaluation program must be evaluated in order to make improvements in receiving feedback, reflecting on the goals and objectives of the program, and developing new ways to succeed. Don't be afraid to embark on pilot programs which may be the result of untested ideas, if program can be improved or positively changed. New challenges of the 21st century will require new methods of teaching, mentoring, and evaluating our successes and failures.

As mentors we must shy away from scaring our young mentees with our "old war stories," as well as understanding our mentees as people, not empty vessels in which information can be "poured." They, like us, must learn through experience, risk-taking and pushing their own limits. Mentors should never lose sight of the goal that the primary reason for character education is to make our world a better place, and helping our young people rise to the leadership potential necessary for the future.

KEY POINTS ABOUT BUILDING CHARACTER

In this chapter we looked at how a strong character and morals both affect how we mentor and how a mentor's good example encourages mentees to act positively. Following are key points to remember about building the character of mentees to achieve success:

1. Character is a multifaceted developmental system rather than a set of traits formed by the outcome of a person's context and experiences, including a synthesis of moral reasoning—an unfinished product which is continuously evolving.

2. The individual components of character can be analyzed, assessed, and taught.

3. The three universal virtues of character are caring, inquisitiveness, and self-control, which are combined with personal, interpersonal, and cultural values.

4. An evaluation program is essential to character development.

CHAPTER

7

Creating a Mentoring Community

We are all connected, interwoven in the intricate web of community. Our actions ripple through the lives of others.

—Desmond Tutu

ALTHOUGH WE HAVE, so far, focused primarily on adult-to-youth mentoring, it comes in all shapes and sizes. There are a variety of mentoring types. Understanding the value of these different types of mentoring formats will help program directors, mentors and protégés of all ages better understand the different roles in the mentoring process and establish a more valuable mentoring opportunity for all.

Mentoring programs can be structured formally or informally. Structured programs frequently match mentors and trainees to one another and provide guidelines and opportunities for volunteers to mentor in a variety of settings and multiple opportunities. Formats for these programs will vary based upon the structure and organization of the group and the program goals. In formal mentoring, program goals generally focus on specific goals identified early in the program and evaluated continuously.

Mentoring programs can be structured ... informally ... [but a] mentoring community *leverages* learning and innovation.

In Sidebar 7.1 on page 142, Prof. M. S. Valiathan shows us how renowned surgeons share and build upon their expertise and innovations, and pass on their experience to successors. Exceptional mentors not only light the path for mentees, they work within a mentoring community, encourage the journey, recognize mentees' accomplishments, and they selflessly build upon the successes of others. A mentoring community *leverages* learning and innovation.

TRADITIONAL MENTORING

There are three types of mentoring that are considered traditional processes: formal mentoring, natural mentoring, and peer-to-peer mentoring. These are examined below.

Formal Mentoring

Formal mentoring provides accountability based on the formal contracts and contacts between the mentors and mentees as well as other involved stakeholders, like parents or program administrators. There are three general types of formal mentoring programs.

Youth mentoring programs in a formal setting usually exist within a school structure or an after school program. Specific goals are outlined for youth development and administrators and staff are usually paid, while mentors are volunteers. These programs can be established in communities, schools, religious organizations, and a wide variety of other sponsoring programs.

Mentors in these programs are adults, providing an adult-to-youth mentoring experience.

Supervisory mentoring typically occurs in the workplace where a direct supervisor also provides support for a new worker in the form of the mentor. In these situations and relationships the supervisor may wear many hats, and perform many, often contradictory roles. Not all supervisors nor employees are comfortable being mentored in this fashion due to the conflicting and intersecting roles.

In many cases it may be more appropriate for supervisor mentees to come from another department, or closely related area but not directly within the department or evaluation chain. This will help to avoid conflicts of interest and provide an opportunity for the employee to have an unbiased "advocate" within the workplace to assist them should the need arise.

Training mentoring can take two forms, that of the formal "trainer-trainee" training under the supervision of a skilled master, who has been tasked to pass knowledge on to the trainee in particular skills. Or, the mentoring relationship may be a more informal one, where peers or near-peers are working to develop skills.

Informal training usually begins in a formal setting and continues beyond the initial training program. Mentees usually return and rely upon their trainers to continue mentoring them as they begin apprenticeship programs and on into their life experience journey. As a result, these mentors will continue to gain skills themselves through the interchange of information.

Natural Mentoring

Another type of mentoring is natural mentoring. This type of program is usually initiated by the mentor, where the mentor observes that a protégé could use some help in developing their skills, capabilities, or interests. Senior mentors reach out to younger mentees in order to provide guidance in a wide variety of settings.

In this relationship the mentor and mentee will have a natural and implicit relationship based upon a common field or area in which they were originally involved, such as the work setting, teachers within the school setting, and university professors as mentors for graduate students within their disciplines.

Peer-to-Peer Mentoring

Peer-to-peer mentoring involves individuals at the same level, and usually within the same field providing skills training to one another. These individuals are usually in similar positions and use the mentoring opportunity to provide support, empathy and advice. This is extremely helpful for individuals in the similar stage of career development, where mentoring can assist in motivating each other and providing opportunities for growth within the workplace.

This is also a natural mentoring process in our schools and universities. One aspect of peer-to-peer mentoring has tradi-tionally been focused on tutoring in particular courses. However, relational mentoring opportunities are often the outcome of these initial encounters.

Reciprocal Mentoring

In many cases, relationships will evolve where neither party is designated as a "mentor." Each person is a confidant and resource to the other person. In these experiences, mentees will share goals and encourage personal accountability. They may also serve as a sounding board for ideas and provide reality checks for future plans.

> In relational mentoring the focus is on establishing either highly structured, long-term mentoring relationship programs that meet specific organizational objectives; or informal, long-term mentoring relationships that are established to assist mentees throughout their lifetimes.

Excellent reciprocal mentoring is having the objectivity necessary for real mentoring. Often times friends and family will not have the skills necessary, nor the objectivity to provide this type of mentoring. Mentoring may also add stress to familial relationships, and therefore professional colleagues may be the best choice for reciprocal mentoring.

RELATIONAL MENTORING

Over the past 30 years, researchers have focused on traditional mentoring, and more particularly on formal and natural mentoring settings, as a means of providing developmental assistance

Sidebar 7.1. A surgeon cuts through conventional wisdom

PROF. M. S. VALIATHAN, SURGEON
Sree Chitra Tirunal Institute for Medical Sciences and Technology, India

The dictionary defines a mentor as an experienced and trusted advisor. The word originated in Greece where Odysseus entrusted a friend with the education of his son Telemachus as a mentor. While all these descriptions are correct, the word "mentor" has acquired, over the years, additional shades of meaning such as guide, leader, ideal and even a Guru. A mentor comprehends all these connotations and his disciple or follower, confronted by a dilemma, would always wonder how the mentor would address the problem as a guide for decision making.

I owe my surgical training of several years to teachers in three continents. As handicraft dominates surgery, surgical training involves more of apprenticeship than pedagogy. Among my surgical teachers, I would regard the late Dr. Charles Hufnagel, Professor of Surgery at the Georgetown University Medical School, Washington D.C. as my mentor. He made surgical history by successfully implanting a prosthetic valve in the descending thoracic aorta in 1952 when open heart surgery was not yet born! He was an exceptionally gifted surgeon with a luminous mind, skillful hands, and infinite capacity for work. He was a supreme individualist who used a heart lung machine, heart valves and vascular grafts designed by him with success throughout his service.

When I joined his program as a resident in 1967, he was fully active and lived up to his reputation as a hard task master. His two residents—a Portuguese surgeon and me—covered his service, which involved the care of patients from all over the United States, assisting him in operations, doing seminars for medical students and taking part in laboratory research.

During the day we were with him while examining patients and talking with them, and he insisted that a physician must acquire special skills in doctor-patient communications. We assisted him during surgical operations every day, learning his masterly technique and trying to imbibe his unflappability in tackling many a crisis during operations and postoperative care. It was not uncommon to assist Hufnagel for six or seven hours at a stretch for elective surgery only to be summoned back for an emergency soon after and find him "scrubbing" cheerfully. When everyone in his team was exhausted, he appeared tireless and cheered the team by his favorite phrase, "upward and onward"!

Hufnagel was however more than a master surgeon who excelled in his surgical panache. He had a luminous mind which threw light on dark patches of surgery where no remedy was visible, but the searchlight of his mind would uncover a stream of novel techniques and devices such as mechanical heart valves, micro

A surgeon cuts through conventional wisdom (continued)

crimped vascular grafts, and a ventricular blood pump.

Following the first human cardiac transplant in 1967 in South Africa by Christian Barnard, another daring surgeon, Hufnagel initiated a project on developing xenografts as an answer to the critical shortage of donor hearts.

Since a porcine heart could perform the hemodynamic function of a human heart, it was believed at that time a porcine heart could be a candidate for transplantation in humans. Hufnagel's project was a preliminary step in that direction in so far as it involved the injection of a guinea pig's thymic material in a rabbit fetus to create a half guinea pig – half rabbit chimera whose organs might escape rejection in guinea pigs.

As I was asked to run the project, I read extensively on transplantation immunology starting with the papers of Robert Good, the father or immunology, and chanced to read the autobiography of Macfarlane Burnet, an eminent virologist. Brilliantly written, he noted that the "self not self" recognition, which underlays rejection, is a product of millions of years of evolution and its reversal or annulment by medical or surgical tricks were inconceivable.

That worried me and I expressed my doubts to Hufnagel during one of our nocturnal dialogues. He told me bluntly:

"The trouble is you read too much. When you read too much and know too much, you weigh pros and cons too much and would prefer to do nothing. Had I taken that road, there would have been no prosthetic valve. All arguments were against it, but my surgical instinct was for it. If you have that instinct, show the daring to do it."

Hufnagel gave me a position in his faculty at Georgetown and helped me in many ways to settle in the U.S. He was upset when I decided to return to India in 1972 and predicted I would regret the decision. Nevertheless, I remained in touch with him throughout my uncertain start in India and arrival in the Chitra Institute where we not only performed open heart surgery successfully but also developed a series of medical devices including a heart valve quite successfully.

When Hufnagel visited Chitra, he saw our cardiac surgical program and took a close look at the work in our medical technology laboratories. As he was stepping out, he told me with a smile, "You know, I didn't quite believe the annual reports you had sent me. Now I have seen your technology development, I still don't believe it."

by more senior individuals, usually within the protégé's organization. This single, binary relationship provides intervention techniques in a specific area and within a specific focus, which may be of a short-term duration.

In relational mentoring the focus is on establishing either highly structured, long-term mentoring relationship programs that meet specific organizational objectives; or informal, long-term mentoring relationships that are established to assist mentees throughout their lifetimes.

In the highly structured long-term format, resources are usually abundant and the grounds are specific to a mentee's needs. The mentee's needs are evaluated and usually determined to be very high in a specific area. Mentors are then given resources necessary to assist the mentees overcome and advance in these areas. These programs have the potential for an intense, although short, and productive mentor-mentee relationship. This type of program may have a succession plan associated with it, allowing relationships to evolve in a variety of ways and for others within a particular group or organization to then step in and take the mentee to the next higher level within their mentoring program.

Long-term, informal programs are usually relationally based and provide an opportunity for the protégé to have a mentor to discuss ideas and problems, to listen and share special knowledge throughout a mentee's lifetime.

In these programs the mentor's resources may or may not be substantial, and the mentee's needs are usually low. In most cases the mentor provides short-term assistance in a particular problem area for advice on a particular strategic path for the mentees. The mentee usually has the time and talents available to move forward, based on this relational program. This is often referred to as "friendship mentoring."

CREATING THE COMMUNITY

Ultimately in our mentoring work we want to connect with peers, as well as mentors, by strengthening our relational mentoring to form a mentoring organization (formal or informal) at the highest level. By doing so we can create a mentoring com-

Sidebar 7.2. We are each individuals within a community

NALIN SURIE, DIRECTOR GENERAL
Indian Council of World Affairs, Iindian Foreign Service

In different stages of my career, from when I was a very young diplomat literally raw and out of a university, and in subsequent years, I have had mentors in stations as diverse as Hong Kong, Brussels, Dar es Salaam, Thimphu, New York (at the United Nations), Warsaw, Beijing, and London.

Based on these experiences, the attributes that I looked for in my mentors included their ability to guide me in applying my theoretical and empirical knowledge to issues that impact or could impact on different aspects of India's foreign and security policies. In addition, what is critical is the trust and confidence that they reposed in me. It is critical for mentors to stand by the individual whom he or she is mentoring.

My mentors literally taught me how to study and analyze a complicated country, to not micromanage my work, to help strengthen my ability to research subjects, and to let me grow and develop both as an individual and an officer. This was possible because my mentors were secure in their own skins and did not need to compete with their younger colleagues.

As time went by, my relationship with my mentors became one of partnership, friendship, trust, respect and as guides who encouraged me in my endeavors while at the same time ensuring that I did not lose sight of the objectives in the effort to resolve problems while maintaining my integrity. When I was going wrong or perhaps getting overconfident they gently, but firmly, made me course correct to ensure I did not stray too far off the track and lose sight of the main purpose: to serve with dignity and confidence.

Yet another critical quality in a mentor is to identify the individual strengths of each person and then use these attributes as part of a plan to achieve required goals. It is critical to remind oneself that every person has some strengths and if those can be utilized, the overall quality and personality of the individual improves.

In my attempt to mentor my younger colleagues while I was in service and subsequently as an independent analyst and member of a think tank, the effort has been to follow the principles that my mentors did. Discussions have to be frank with those you are mentoring and you have to be able to take your share of criticism when they disagree with you.

Lastly, mentees have to know that it is their work that will be recognized. Only then can trust be built between the mentor and mentee.

munity enabling us to connect with peers and mentors of all ages and stages who can help us thrive.

Cecilia Sanchez and Anya Brown created just such a community at the University of Georgia in Athens where they are doctoral candidates (Sanchez). The program helped to provide support groups for women in science, as well as recruit new minorities and underrepresented groups within the University.

Creating a mentoring community is extremely important as research suggests that up to 95% of mentoring relationships are informal, where the individual selects a person by whom they would like to be mentored. Relationships generally develop naturally and may not even be identified as "mentoring." Within a thriving mentoring community relationships tend to form and grow, gradually moving over a period of time, usually 3 to 6 years. However, some mentoring relationships will last a lifetime.

Within a mentoring community, mentors should expect the mentees to be the lead in the development process. Both parties may agree on the mentoring outcomes either verbally or in writing. In most cases the program will be initiated by the mentee. Informal mentoring activity should not conflict with productivity of either the mentees or the mentors. Within the structure care must be taken to ensure that each has the appropriate amount of time available and willingness to engage in the mentoring process.

Community mentoring also provides an opportunity for networking, as well as providing a variety of role models whose behaviors, attitudes, and strategies can be emulated to achieve success, as Nalin Surie shares with us in Sidebar 7.2 page 145.

While mentees should not become clones of anyone else, role model mentoring does provide opportunities for the mentee to observe all types of behaviors and to adapt those most suitable, while ignoring those that may be less effective. Role modeling involves identifying people mentees believe are operating in a positive and effective way, noticing how they do particular skills and how they interact with others around them.

■ ■ ■

KEY POINTS ABOUT MENTORING COMMUNITIES

Although mentoring can, and often does, happen "naturally" in informal, individual relationships, it is most effective and enduring within a "formal" community and with a supportive program. Following are key points to remember about mentoring communities:

1. Both formal and informal mentoring programs can be effective in providing the mentoring experience.

2. "Traditional mentoring" consists of *formal* mentoring programs; and *natural* mentoring in which an implicit relationship based upon a common field or area, such as a work or school setting, or provides the basis for peer-to-peer mentoring.

3. Relational Mentoring, in which a relationship is formed in a specific area and within a specific focus of organizational objectives or informal relationships are becoming more popular.

8

National and Professional Programs

The key to a thriving professional program lies in building strong relationships, fostering collaboration, and constantly innovating.

—Richard Branson

MANY ORGANIZATIONS HAVE for years developed, organized and employed formal mentoring programs as a means of promoting positive aspects of development and avoiding potential problem behaviors. This has expanded in recent years to the development of a variety of formal national and international mentoring programs. While each program is developed to enhance specific behaviors that foster achievement of goals unique to the organization or group, there are common program characteristics.

Common elements of formal mentoring programs include

elements of the organizational structure, as well as specific components related to mentee goals and mentee behaviors. A strong formal mentoring structure establishes ground rules for the program and identifies specific leadership roles, processes and procedures, including emergency procedures should the need arise, financial performance, risk management, and ultimately mentee performance assessments.

A formal mentoring structure begins with a Senior Mentoring Advisory Group (SMAG). The Senior Mentoring Advisory Group provides vision and leadership for the overall mentoring program. Members of the MAG are selected from the component organizations providing the overall mentoring leadership for the program.

MISSION AND VISION

The Senior Mentoring Advisory Group provides vision and leadership and defines the mission of the mentoring program into which each mentor can contribute. Development of the mission and vision and the values program represents need to be more than just a quickly listed group of characteristics. Senior leaders must believe in what these items represent and ensure that all stakeholders understand and uphold the same values, vision for the future, and mission goals. These must be actively promoted on a daily basis. The best way to do this is to make sure that senior leaders are present and advocating directly to all administrators, staff, mentors and mentees the value the program.

Financial Responsibilities

Another function of the Senior Mentoring Advisory Group is to provide needed financial resources for the program. Their role is to provide specific expertise as well as policymaker access.

Each organizational program will be different based upon the established vision, mission, and goals of the program. However, key factors must be clearly identified. There are a variety of important questions to be considered and answered by the group to help in framing the program. These include thoughts on reputational development of the program, financial leadership and performance, risk management and performance assessments.

> The SMAG also serves as the *fiduciary body* for the program ... [with] oversight of funds ... [and] fund-raising activities.

An SMAG also serves as the *fiduciary body* for the program. They should be the connections to potential funders, as well as providing legal advice, and expertise as needed. Financial leadership requires appropriate oversight of funds, and includes checks and balances on expenditures, as well as integration of fund-raising activities. Each of these activities have legal ramifications that must be understood and carried out by the senior advisory management group.

The authors recommend that the Senior Mentoring Advisory Group includes legal expertise to avoid legal and financial pitfalls. Financial management is a very important element of the program and structure and can greatly affect the program's success, but a more detailed discussion is beyond the scope of this book.

Defining Success for the Program

One of the first elements to consider in the program development is defining success.

To define success, the leadership must first envision what

Sidebar 8.1. Fly a kite and go for the moon

R. A. MASHELKAR, FORMER DIRECTOR GENERAL
Council of Scientific and Industrial Research, India

I have been a mentee and I have mentored a number of young scientists and innovators as well as science and innovation leaders. Four guiding principles have helped me:

First, I believe everyone is someone. Everyone has potential. A mentor's first responsibility is to see as to how the mentee could reach his true potential, and having reached that, how can he exceed that.

My favorite story that I often used to inspire mentees was about the conquest of Mount Everest, earth's highest mountain. I used to remind them that until Tenzing Norgay and Edmund Hillary conquered Everest in 1953, the feat was considered to be impossible. But once it was shown that it was possible, there have been close to 6000 conquests! And seemingly impossible feats have been done: Someone has climbed Everest 21 times; it has been climbed without supplemental oxygen; an 80-year old, a young boy, and a young girl (each less than 14 years old) have climbed it, as have a blind person, a double leg amputee, and a double arm amputee. If they could do it, you can too.

Second, it's extremely important for a mentor to be positive. I always used to emphasize that an innovator is one who sees what everyone else sees but thinks of what no one else does. Such a person has to be curious, which leads to creativity, which leads to a new creation.

Third, never tell a mentee what to do, but how to do it, so the mentee learns by doing. Taking risks and possibly failing is an obvious part of learning. I give a different definition of the world: to "fail" is the "first attempt to learn."

Fourth, a mentor has to be a trusted advisor. It takes time to build trust. And a mentor has to be an active listener and open minded, with a great deal of emotional intelligence and empathy. He has to also lead by example. So, while telling mentees that they should take risks, I tell them how I took risks, not only when doing my own science, but also when teaching science.

As the Director of the National Chemical Laboratory, I created the spirit of risk-taking by innovative funding mechanisms. I created a "Kite Flying Fund" where audacious ideas would be supported. I set aside one percent of my research budget for supporting any idea that had a one-in-a-thousand chance of success. The signal was that dreaming and failure are not a crime.

Later, as Director General of the Council of Scientific and Industrial Research, which comprised of 40 national laboratories, I created a similar "New Idea Fund" with a similar objective.

Finally, the concept went nationwide in 2000 with the New Millennium Indian Technology Leadership Initiative to make Indian technology lead and not follow. We were busy creating products that

Fly a kite and go for the moon (continued)

were first to India but not first to the world. Creating ideas that were first to the world meant creating ideas that were never tried before.	So, the possibility of potential failure was built into the NMITLI funding mechanism. And the results were again amazing!

their program's success will look like. It needs to address questions about the program, like—

- What would the group like the program's ultimate reputation to be?

- What is the ultimate outcome?

- How best can it be achieved?

From there the team can work backwards to identify key milestones and integration points to build the reputation of the program. Evaluations and assessments will be an integral part of development of these milestones. Build with the future in mind.

Reputation will be an outcome of your program success. Warren Buffett once said, "It takes 20 years to build a reputation and about five minutes to ruin it." Every stakeholder in the program must understand and look for problem areas which could detract from the overall reputation.

Program differentiation must be considered before milestones can be developed. The SMAG will need to differentiate their mentoring program from all others with questions like—

- What will be the novelty of the mentoring program?

- What will set the program apart of other programs?

- Why should mentors and mentees be a part of this organizational program?

- What are the benefits and outcomes to be derived from the program?

Sidebar 8.2. Chasing anomalies for lessons and discoveries

V. S. Ramamurthy, Secretary
Department of Science and Technology, Government of India

My first experience with a mentor was in 1964 when I joined the Fission Physics Group headed by Dr. Raja Ramanna in the then Atomic Energy Establishment, in Trombay, India, that is the present Bhabha Atomic Research Centre. Those were hard days. The resources were limited. Foreign exchange was scarce. Nuclear instruments were not available off-the-shelf. We had to design and build our own detectors, pre-amplifiers, amplifiers, pulse analysis systems, data recording systems etc. Travel and communications were expensive and often unaffordable. There was always a lurking fear whether we could do competitive research with all these constraints

We learned a lot from Dr. Ramanna, though. At the outset, he would say: "Do your best and have faith in yourself. Think horizontally. Vertical thinking is subject to constraints of all kinds." He was not a "safe science" man. He always dared to differ. If I went to him and said "I have carried out this measurement and my results agree with all previous measure-ments" he would reply: "Congrat-ulations. You have a done a good job, but this is not a problem in which to spend more time." If, on the other hand, I said "I have carried out this measurement and I have a problem reconciling my results with other existing mea-surements" his response was "Very good, double check your measure-ments. If the discrepancy persists, this is where you should concen-trate." In Ramanna's view, discrep-ancies and anomalies are possible precursors of new information.

Chasing anomalies was Raman-na's working principle, and it yielded many successes for us. The rapid vanishing of shell effects with excitation energy, the postu-lation of pre-equilibrium fission in heavy ion fusion-fission reactions and the entrance channel effects in heavy ion fusion reactions are all our responses to anomalies seen in the experimental data. All our con-jectures have stood the test of time and are now widely accepted. But it was Ramanna's insistence for exploring outliers and anomalies that lead us to discoveries.

The value of the responses must then be conveyed to each and every stakeholder in the program. More importantly, each stakeholder must buy in to the program at every level.

In Sidebar 8.1 on page 152 R. A. Mashelkar gives us an example of a mentoring program that differentiated from others and taught important lessons by embracing risk. It shows what intrepid scientists can do rather than pursue "safe science."

Mashelkar encouraged mentees to explore outlier ideas on the chance that one in a thousand such "crazy" ideas might just be a significant discovery. If nothing else, it inculcated in mentees the importance of not fearing failure, which Sidebar 3.2 on page 60 also illustrates.

In Sidebar 8.2 on page 154 V. S. Ramamurthy argues that safe science is worthwhile for learning fundamentals, but only repeats what is already known. Discoveries lie in the unknown, in the data that is in disagreement and requires further exploration by a curious and persistent mind, oftentimes encouraged by a mentor.

Many of the world's scientific breakthroughs were once considered crazy—or heretical. Proponents of the middle ages like Giordano Bruno and Galileo were persecuted or put to death for contradicting the doctrines of their times. Still, their critical thinking and courage advanced science and civilizations.

Today's mentors need to encourage tomorrow's pioneers to be willing to experiment outside the envelopes of conventional wisdom.

The Mentoring Environment

Although mentoring takes place in many different locations and with many different people, senior mentoring groups must be cognizant of and emphasize the importance of the mentoring environment. This includes relationships among administrators, staff, mentors and mentees, and not just the mentors and mentees themselves.

- Where will the mentoring take place?

- Will the formal program provide formal facilities for mentoring, and if so are they welcoming and appropriate for both the mentor and mentee?

- If mentoring activities will be taking place off-site, are there any limits in locations of which mentors and mentees need to be aware?

- Will mentoring program include both formal and informal mentoring activities?

Implementation of any program requires a risk management assessment. SMAGs will need to understand and thoroughly evaluate key questions such as—

- What are the risks involved in developing a formal mentoring program?

- What identified risks are acceptable, and how can these risks be mitigated?

- What identified risks can be managed, and who would be the best persons to do so?

- What risks are absolutely unacceptable to the program, and how can these be mitigated or eliminated?

Training Programs for Mentors

The senior leadership must also identify and develop a training program for the mentors. This ensures the mentors are focused on the outcomes and have the tools available to be successful.

Mentors must recognize and encourage the potential of their mentees. In many cases mentoring will involve mentees joining new communities with different values, conventions, and beliefs. The mentor must understand the process of transition as their mentees distance themselves from past convictions, behaviors, situations, and thinking, while adapting to their new environments. This includes new cultural norms and quite often, multicultural perspectives.

Preliminary mentor assessment is also critical to the outcome of the program. One-on-one mentoring may not always meet the needs of the mentee, so mentors must be adaptable in different mentoring situations.

Even one-on-one mentoring situations require discernment. Do the mentors have the temperament, patience and skills necessary to developing lasting relationships with their mentees? Mentors must be trained and accepting of a mentoring network designed to be a "network of belonging" (Parks 135).

An open mentoring environment in which mentees feel safe will facilitate consideration of different mentee perspectives and a more rapid transition to their new, dynamic environment (Evans).

While the Senior Management Advisory Group sets the vision for the program, it is the Mentoring Program Management Team that puts the vision into action.

THE MENTORING PROGRAM MANAGEMENT TEAM

The Mentoring Program Management Team (MPMT) provides the day-to-day operation of the program. They are responsible for the evaluation and selection of mentors and mentees as well as their continued performance. The MPMT is the first line of conflict resolution for the program

The MPMT will also need to develop and plan program actions and activities, and provide ongoing staff and mentor training. This includes establishing the evaluation criteria for the overall program, collecting data, analyzing the program performance and presenting their analysis to the SMAG.

Performance Assessments

For the program to survive and blossom, program standards and mentor-mentee relationships must be assessed, feedback provided, and the program enhanced. For every program, the frontline supervisors and leaders must clearly define what constitutes success and how that success will be measured.

In developing a program's unique performance assessment, consider the following questions:

- How will success be defined?

- How will performance be assessed?

- What evaluation tools will be used?

- What is the program baseline?

- What policies and practices must be implemented to maximize performance?

One important and often overlooked element common to all mentoring programs is the role of time and termination of the mentoring relationship (McQuillin and Lyons).

The Importance of Time

For mentoring relationships to properly develop into effective programs, researchers have identified the element of time as a critical component. When mentoring relationships are prematurely terminated, mentoring progress often reverses rather than remaining at the static endpoint. In one research study, researchers identified the loss of a mentoring relationship as causing psychological discomfort, as might be expected and being manifested by sadness, and disappointment. Depending upon the mentee's age and maturity level this could also result in confusion and disappointment, as well as anger resulting in significant behavioral changes (Spencer "'It's not'").

It is important to understand why mentor—mentee relationships may end prematurely (usually less than 6-months into the mentoring program. Programs where mentors and their protégés have been mismatched are more likely to end prematurely, especially in youth programs. In youth programs, studies have shown that older adolescents are more likely to prematurely terminate a mentoring relationship.

Additional youth risk factors such as problems in school, alcohol or drug use, mental health issues, or engaging in illegal activities are all potential indicators where the mentee—mentor relationship may end prematurely (Grossman and Rhodes). These relationships must be closely monitored throughout the mentoring process.

Researchers have also identified additional reasons why the mentoring process may lead to premature termination. Changes in life circumstances such as divorce, marriage, birth of a child, loss of a child, loss of income or other factors may lead to disruptions in the mentoring relationship. Dissatisfaction or disinterest over time may also lead to premature termination of the mentoring relationship before it has had time to effectively mature into a beneficial relationship (Spencer; Kupersmidt).

> When mentoring relationships are prematurely terminated, mentoring progress often reverses rather than remaining at the static endpoint. … [M]entor training can positively impact the mentoring relationship resulting in longer-lasting relationships.

Another very important element is mentor abandonment, whether real or imagined. This could be due to a variety of reasons including death of the mentor, disinterest by the mentor in the relationship, or an initial mismatch of mentor and mentee causing loss the caring relationship.

Researchers have identified that mentor training can positively impact the mentoring relationship resulting in longer-lasting relationships (McQuillin et al.). Well trained mentors will impact the success of mentoring programs, as well as the potential for their protégés to seek future mentoring relationships.

We provide additional information on mentor selection and pairing, as well as mentoring training programs in Chapter "9".

NATIONAL PERSPECTIVE OF THE MENTORING PROGRAM

While we have focused on the elements of traditional mentoring programs, we now consider potential national mentoring programs. These programs have applicability in any country. As globalization increases, we encourage readers to consider mentoring from an international perspective where cultures may be quite different from their own current environments.

Looking to the future, most countries and companies will need a mentoring program developed through multi-level, multi-stage models to reach diverse populations. The mentoring community can be built through strategic planning and careful expansion. And the entire effort must be informed through evidence based research of existing mentoring models practiced internationally and in the country, region, across cultures and different knowledge domains.

Traditional mentoring practiced within specific cultures will continue to provide useful pointers to strengthen these programs.

Challenges and Opportunities for National Mentoring

The challenges and opportunities for national mentoring are plentiful. Research points out that mentoring practices in most developing countries are currently isolated, relatively small and regionally specific. There is an imperative need to learn from the current practices and build mentoring programs based on national and international experience. The initial pace of expansion into international perspective programs can be slow, requring close monitoring of the quality of the mentoring program. Success achieved during the initial phase can give the program the necessary momentum to upscale through carefully selected collaborators from across the country and the world.

[M]entoring practices in most developing countries are currently isolated, relatively small and regionally specific. [We] need to learn from the current practices and build mentoring programs based on national and international experience ... for future national and corporate economic successes.

Periodic sharing of experiences, documentation, and analysis to understand the patterns are key to developing of the national model for mentoring. Flexibility for innovation is critical to enhance the quality of the mentoring program.

Researchers in a number of universities across the globe are continuing to address national and international mentoring issues across multicultural societies. These research studies will provide important insights into the development of future national and international mentoring programs. The one thing we do know is that national and international mentoring programs will become essential for future national and corporate economic successes.

Effectively Managing a Program

The cornerstone of a mentoring program is its policy and procedures manual, providing governance and guidance for delivery of mentoring services. The purpose of these written policies
and procedures is to provide short-term guidance and long-term
stability and safety to the program.

Details within the policy procedure manual provide step-by-
step instructions on how to administer and manage the mentoring program within the clearly defined staff roles, our mentoring
expectations, and routine operating guidelines.

In addition, one of the most important aspects of the policy
and procedure manual is the risk management plan. The risk
management plan provides clear and explicit instructions on
how every part of mentoring program will be administered. By
addressing risks up front, the program staff will be able to elim-
inate uncertainties and execute the program in a safe and effective, as well as consistent manner.

> The cornerstone of a mentoring program
> is its policy and procedures manual,
> providing governance and guidance for
> delivery of mentoring services.

While we do not anticipate rapid turnover of key staff, the
policy and procedures manual will provide a source document
for training and orientation of new personnel without losing
crucial program operations knowledge. This in turn, will assist
the program in providing continuity of service and assist the
leadership, mentors, and mentees in conducting and participating in the program.

As the program continues to improve and expand, use of the policy and procedure manual for the program will enable expansion and replication. The written policies contained within the policy and procedure manual are provided to assist members in applying for new grants, following written policies and procedures, standardizing the program, and providing a venue for continued growth. In addition, the policy and procedure manual will provide a baseline for continuous improvement.

Policies and Procedures Defined

Policies and procedures are essentially the set of operating rules and principles under which the program functions. These policies and procedures represent the sum total of decisions, requirements and activities needed to run the mentoring program. All major program rules and guiding principles are captured within the official policies and procedures, and organized within the manual for easy access.

The difference in policies and procedures can quickly be summed up. Policies are high-level program statements that embrace the goals the program and define what is acceptable to ensure program success, the safety of youth in the program, as well as the effective and consistent program operations.

Procedures on the other hand, are statements that describe how specific operational functions are implemented and managed within the program. These procedures are listed as brief statements describing step-by-step processes necessary to implement policies and other agency practices. Within these pages the procedures will include exactly who should carry out specific tasks, and timelines for completion of these tasks.

■ ■ ■

KEY POINTS ABOUT PROGRAMS

This chapter focuses on the requirements and benefits of formalized, national and professional programs that draw from the varied mentoring approaches we covered in previous chapters. Following are key points to remember about national and professional mentoring programs:

1. Formal, structured mentoring programs have been in practice for years, but require buy-in from each stakeholder at every level of the program in order to derive maximum benefits of the mentoring.

2. Mentors must understand the process of transition as mentees distance themselves from past convictions, behaviors, situations, and thinking while adapting to new environments, including new cultural norms and multicultural perspectives.

3. National mentoring programs in many countries are beginning to take shape but provide different challenges and opportunities. Research into national mentoring is ongoing. National and international mentoring programs will become essential for future national and corporate economic success.

4. Clearly written policies and procedures provide the "operating rules and principles" upon which national and professional programs are built. Stakeholders must understand and support these rules and principles.

P A R T

III

Mentoring Experiences and the Future

This section discusses what is required to institute and manage mentoring programs, and what we can expect into the future, including:

- best mentoring practices, evaluations, and case studies,

- how mentors can build relationships with protégés,

- currently available and anticipated mentoring tools,

- mentoring gifted protégés, and

- mentoring challenges now and in the future as we evolve to integrate the virtual and outer spaces as mentoring tools.

9

Best Practices and Methods for Evaluation

Effective evaluation practices are essential to measure progress, inform decision-making, and drive improvement.

—Michael Quinn Patton

M ENTORING IS NOT new, so there is a large volume of information available to organizations to adopt. Mentoring research is also advancing, so groups may need to establish new rules and procedures enhanced by learning from best practices and methods of evaluation of other programs. As such, we provide the following information concerning best practices from a variety of programs around the world.

TARGETED RECRUITMENT AND SCREENING

Previous research has indicated that not all volunteers may be a good fit for the demands of a mentoring relationship. They may have varying backgrounds of their own in terms of closeness and education of the mentoring process with new students. By the same token, not all youth are in the same state of mind from which they can benefit from a mentoring relationship. As such, each mentor, as well as each student must be evaluated independently, and matched in terms of their expectations for the program and stage of both mentoring and learning development.

Mentors recruited for a mentoring program must be both safe and suitable for their mentoring role. Matching mentors with students is of critical importance to make sure a youth's needs are in alignment with the resources that a particular mentor can provide.

Mentoring programs should not be overly restrictive. Mentoring programs should not be very narrowly applied to only handpicked groups of special mentors and students. However, programs do need to ensure that the populations they serve, and the volunteers who are forming those relationships, will likely have a successful mentoring experience.

If at any time there is a question about the relationship, program administrative personnel must identify the issues and determine immediately if a new mentor is necessary for a particular youth.

Training Programs

For a program to be successful, everyone involved in the program must understand and be administering—and learning under the program—from the same set of rules.

Customized training must be provided for mentors, youth, administrators, parents, and others who may have a role in both matching mentors and students, as well as conducting the mentoring activities. Training must be identified based on the individual program goals, as well as expected activities and interactions.

[N]ot all volunteers may be a good fit for the demands of a mentoring relationship. … Mentors … must be both safe and suitable for their mentoring role. Matching mentors with students is of critical importance to make sure a youth's needs are in alignment with … a particular mentor.

Mentors will lead specific training on their mentees' circumstances, strengths, and challenges. Regardless of the program and situation, mentors can expect to be tested by their mentees in a variety of ways as the relationship evolves. Mentors must learn coping skills and strategies for overcoming barriers. By doing so program administrators will significantly increase the odds of their mentors making it through many of the challenges of mentoring, and have a long, successful match with their mentees.

While program goals and settings differ, all mentors should be trained in youth development principles, listening and communication skills, and the role of the mentor. Additional topics can be included over time as the need arises.

Mentees and their parents should also be provided pre-match training through an orientation and potentially more detailed workshops in order to prepare them for the work that lies ahead. Their role and interactions with their mentees will mean the difference between the program's success or failure, so it is essential that mentees understand the goals of the program and how mentoring mentors will be attempting to implement strategies for their effective learning.

Matching, Monitoring, Supervision and Retention

Recruitment and pre-match preparations mean little if the programs are not making sound matches and monitoring them properly over time throughout the mentoring relationship. Programs should develop a set of matching criteria consisting of such attributes as common mentor/mentee interests, compatibility of meeting times and locations, similar personal backgrounds, and such considerations as culture, religion, and gender.

Matches should be monitored at least monthly in the first months and quarterly thereafter, assuming that the match is progressing as planned. These checks should involve the mentor, youth, and parents to make sure that all parties are happy with the process and that any issues can be immediately addressed.

Consistent meetings of mentors and mentees must be maintained throughout the year. In many cases academic programs will dictate the need for additional mentoring sessions.

Another key element of excellent mentoring programs is a retention strategy. Retention strategies identify rewards and honors for all participants for the hard work that they do in the program and serve both as a means of recognition and an opportunity to really recruit the best mentors for continuous mentoring activities.

At the end of all phases of the program, closure procedures should be implemented to leave all participants satisfied with the outcome of the program.

Mentoring relationships end for many reasons, some good and others not. However, it is important that each ending go through an appropriate closure process. The process should be designed to let all participants reflect on the experience, process their feelings about it, and hopefully leave the program on a positive note.

It is especially important for young people to feel that the experience was valuable and positive, as it will greatly influence how they approach other relationships with adults, other mentors, and mentoring programs throughout their future (Miller "Best Practices").

In a final word about matching, peer mentoring programs may want to place extra emphasis on match supervision to mitigate potential negative role modeling that can happen when peer mentors deviate from program guidelines.

Process and Outcome Evaluation

The best mentoring programs are under constant analysis and enhancement of their services. It is essential to have an established feedback process for monitoring, evaluating, correcting, and reevaluating the programs, goals, and objectives, as well as evaluating both the mentors and mentees (and perhaps even administrators and parents).

Program evaluation can highlight aspects of service delivery that need improvement, demonstrate the usefulness of mentoring strategies or program curriculum, as well as provide evidence of success to funding sources and generate other qualitative and quantitative results that can be used in marketing, recruitment, and sustainability activities.

Administrative Staff

The administrative staffs of programs are often overlooked. Since one of the greatest challenges for many youth organizations is staff turnover, mentoring programs must be formulated to be resilient and robust so that fluctuations in administrative staff do not disrupt the program. Mentoring programs are often quite small, using only one or two paid staff members and rotating many volunteers through it.

Disruption in services when a program coordinator leaves can be substantial. Program leadership should do what they can to minimize turnover and provide ongoing professional development opportunities to their practitioners, which can keep them up to date on the latest concepts in mentoring and help the program maintain an even keel even in times of turbulence.

Stability of Funding

Nothing can sour a community on mentoring more than having a trusted program close its doors due to a funding crisis. Sustainability planning and resource development are critical components of running an effective program.

Adequate funding must be provided to allow programs to operate with full staff; pay for special activities, such as outings for the youth or volunteer recognition events; and keep the program from having to cut corners and how services are delivered.

The Logic Model

Youth mentoring programs should also develop a logic model that can drive program evaluation, providing a roadmap to understanding which parts the program may need refinement over time. This is essential as evaluations may dictate multiple modifications and expansions of the program depending on population served and the goals of the program. A living logic model will provide a pathway to program success.

RELATIONSHIP BEST PRACTICES

The focus on the preceding paragraphs has been on best practices for structural components of a mentoring program. However, a mentoring program's linchpin is its relationship structure. In this regard, we provide the following best practices at the relationship level.

The Developmental Approach

Current research indicates that the best mentoring relationships develop most easily when mentors take a broad youth developmental approach. The goal of the relationship, of course, is mutuality, trust, and empathy formed during the relationship that provides a basis for internal change within the mentees.

To foster this type of relationship, a mentor must not be overly focused on *prescriptive* actions, or those activities that will "fix" the young person's "problems." Mentors must focus on building a close relationship early in the process and maintain that closeness throughout the relationship. Mentors must keep in mind that, above all else, they are there to help the youth find their own paths and their own voices.

Mentors must be consistent and committed to the mentoring process. There is a clear relationship between the consistency of mentors, the relationship longevity, and positive outcomes and influence on the mentees. Don't worry about building the big program instantly as rapport with the mentee will lead to program success. However, mentors must avoid any negativity on their mentees. This works best when the mentors understand completely their role—mentors are there for the mentees!

Mentors must be dedicated to a role model of sharing ideas, listening effectively, and communicating effectively to the mentee, while providing stability to the mentee and the program.

Limits of Mentoring

By its very nature, mentoring is a limited role. Mentors should not get drawn into family conflicts, nor focused on "fixing" the child's circumstances, or providing help beyond the limits of what the program can support.

In general, mentors are not psychologists, teachers, or social workers. Although they have specialties and skills which they can bring to bear in the mentoring circumstances, they cannot, nor should they even try, to substitute for these professionals. Each has a role to play in the life of a mentee. A mentor's role is to guide them to the appropriate support and help, and constantly be the mentee's "trusted friend."

[M]entoring is a limited role. Mentors should not get drawn into … providing help beyond the limits of what the program can support.

To maintain this trusted friend role, mentors must work effectively with program staff, parents, and other stakeholders in the relationship. If mentors are to be successful, they must make sure to support one another and that the role they are playing is not deviating from, but rather is working with, the support provided by other organizations, other mentors, and other professionals. The first and foremost link for mentors is to maintain open lines of communication with everyone involved in the program.

Mentoring Activities

Once mentors and mentees have been assigned, it's time to get acquainted and talk in general terms to discover "Who am I working with?" as well as explore ideas for the mentoring relationship to grow. That is the time to take charge and get to know the assigned protégé.

For the mentor, keep in mind that mentoring is not just another meeting or program! You are now opening a relationship. Like all relationships it must be built on a solid foundation and continually nurtured. How do you quickly establish a solid foundation?

Time spent doing things together in "mentoring moments" will provide significant payoff in building relationships and changing the lives of both mentors and mentees. The key to effective mentoring is "layering" mentoring times in conversations. This will provide a less intimidating atmosphere for the mentee and provide opportunities for the mentor to observe the relationship in progress and to explore other opportunities for success as they arise. These types of mentoring activities are far more useful than a single, "big meeting" in which you mentors meet mentees only superficially.

There are thousands of ideas for activities. To find something that both a mentor and mentee are interested in, they must initiate and explore ways to enhance that interest. One excellent source of activities for youth to start with was created by three authors— Linda Phillips-Jones, Jean Ann Walth, and Carlo Walth—that literally offers a hundred such ideas.

Luckily, mentoring is not new. Thousands, if not millions, of mentors and mentees have gone before us and have provided researchers with keys to enhance a variety of foundation-building activities. Other mentors have paved the way for us by providing information from interviews and observations that will enhance your program.

Most of the ideas presented will require active involvement and should take place during your official mentoring meetings. However, be prepared to seize the moment as other activities and interactions become available. Keep in mind that mentoring does not stop just because the meetings have ended. This is a relationship. Continue to build upon it. One way to do so is to also use mentoring activities and ideas independently, with the mentees conducting activities and then "reporting-in" when you meet again for the official mentoring sessions.

Mentoring activities should be a central element of the mentor-mentee relationship. Use your ingenuity and discover how you can make the relationship between mentor and mentee a strong one.

Additional Resources

Additional resources concern mentoring and evaluation programs can be found in a variety of locations. Readers are encouraged to do as much work as possible in understanding the mentoring process, their mentoring role, and mentoring programs, before during and even after a stint as a mentor. Keep in mind that mentoring crosses many disciplines, and available resources may be found in psychology, learning development, mentoring and other related programs.

■ ■ ■

KEY POINTS ABOUT EVALUATIONS

In this chapter we discussed the particular stresses and issues that youthful mentees experience during their physical, intellectual, social, and emotional development. Following are key points to remember about mentees in this age group:

1. For formal mentoring programs to be most effective mentors must be targeted for recruitment, screened to provide the most desirable capabilities and values, and trained for the circumstances, strengths, and challenges of the program.

2. For formal programs, funding stability is essential for sustainability and effectiveness of the program.

3. Mentor-protégé relationships are the linchpin to effective mentoring and must be consistently developed to provide mutuality, trust, and empathy.

4. The nature of mentor-protégé relationships must, by necessity, contain limitations for the mentor.

10

Case Studies as an Educational Tool

Case studies are a powerful educational tool that bridges the gap between theory and practice, engaging students in real-life scenarios and developing critical thinking skills.

— John Dewey

A VARIETY OF ANECDOTES appear as brief case studies throughout this book to highlight points made in the prose. In this chapter, we provide two detailed case studies and analyze in depth these real situations encountered by experienced mentors and educators. We start by providing a generic tool for analysis of the case studies, followed by the actual case study scenarios.

A case study presents an account of what happened to an individual or group of individuals over a number of years. It chronicles events that individuals had to deal with, providing a rich environment of research information concerning the complex study in a condensed package.

Case studies prove valuable for several reasons. First, case studies provide mentors with an opportunity to evaluate a mentoring situation that can briefly demonstrate many of the lessons learned of mentoring research staff, as well as lifetimes of mentoring experience in order to demonstrate effective mentoring methodologies, student/mentee learning methodologies, and both ineffective and effective ways of managing the results.

By reading and analyzing case studies, the mentor will, in a relatively short period of time, have the chance to appreciate the problems faced by other mentors and understand some effective means of dealing with these real-life situations.

In addition, case studies can illustrate what you have learned. The meaning and the implication of this information can be made clearer when it is applied to case studies. Both theory and concepts in case studies reveal what is actually happening in life and allow the mentor to evaluate solutions that other mentors have adopted. Consequently, when you analyze cases, you must become a detective, who uses a set of conceptual tools and probes what happened, who was responsible and why, by evaluating evidence provided in the case study.

[W]hen you analyze cases, you must become a detective, who uses a set of conceptual tools and probes what happened, who was responsible and why, by evaluating evidence provided in the case study.

These case studies provide an excellent opportunity for mentors to test their problem-solving abilities with real-world circumstances prior to actually encountering and working with a mentee. But case studies are not just for mentors; mentees also learn from their own experiences and that of others. This chapter is useful to both.

It's important to remember that in most cases there are no right answers, as several methods may be applied and lead to the same results. However, case studies will sharpen a mentor's capacity to understand and apply a variety of theories and concepts.

Case studies also provide mentors an opportunity to participate in group discussions and gain additional experience by presenting ideas to others. Experienced mentors can use these case studies to work with younger mentors to evaluate their readiness for entry into more challenging mentoring situations.

In open discussions, mentors can organize their views and thoughts, as well as conclusions on particular methodologies in mentoring and present them to other mentors in a classroom setting. In nearly all cases other mentors will analyze the same issues differently, forcing the mentors to argue their points and be willing to accept alternative conclusions.

Be prepared for debate! This is how mentoring will be in the real world, as mentees may or may not respond to your chosen mentoring methodology.

Working in groups to analyze the following case studies will afford mentors the opportunity to learn about the group process involved, multiple perspectives of the cases presented, and enable mentors to practice their team skills. As you work in groups, be aware that both time and allocated responsibility for the case analysis may not be equally shared among the group members. Some group members will shirk their responsibilities and other group members will be so self-assured of their own ideas that they will try to dominate the group's analysis.

Do not be afraid to voice your opinions. More importantly all members should be accepting of other ideas within the group. This is the only way that mentors will be able to grow.

KEYS TO EFFECTIVE ANALYSIS

To assist in your analysis of the case studies, the authors provide the following steps which may be useful to consider in evaluating the case material. Let these be your guide for your "deductive" exercises.

1. Analyze the individual's history, development and growth. Which areas may have signaled different patterns for growth? Were these areas identified by others? If so, how are they identified, and how did teachers, parents, or other mentors respond?

2. Analyze the mentee's character, whether it changed over time. Was character a helpful or detrimental factor in the mentee's progression or success? How?

3. Analyze and discuss alternative learning styles presented in the case studies. Analyze the mindset at different times of the mentee's experience and if it affected the mentee's learning.

4. Analyze examples of effective and ineffective teaching, parenting, and mentoring.

5. Analyze the external environment. Was the school environment restrictive for this individual? Was it open, allowing individual learning and growth? Was the home environment conducive to promote independent learning? Did the home provide additional resources as part of the cultural capital? What were they? What role did it play in promoting knowledge advancement in the individual?

6. Describe if a mentoring community and/or if a national or professional program played a significant role and how.

7. Identify a particular catalyst that set the stage for maximizing the student potential. How could you as a mentor have provided this catalyst, or perhaps a different one?

8. Analyze and discuss the role of education, and the teacher's role in mentoring.

9. Analyze and discuss the role of parents as role models and mentors for their children.

10. Analyze and discuss the student's behaviors. Which behaviors provided obstacles for the student to overcome, and why? Which behaviors were most effective in changing the student's learning outcomes? What other behaviors may be displayed by other students in similar situations?

11. Analyze the role of communications and technologies in the case study. Provide examples of positive or negative communications or use of technologies.

12. Discuss the role of moral courage by all players in the case study. Define moral courage. Did anyone in the case study demonstrate particularly strong moral courage? If so, how?

Make some recommendations as to how you as a mentor would have interceded in the case study had you been involved as a mentor. And finally, have fun with these case studies, open your mind to new ideas, and be prepared to evaluate your mentoring opportunities with the same open-mindedness.

In the following two case studies, we enumerate a detailed, real profile of an individual for analysis. These two successful stories illustrate effective interventions, and provide examples of persistence in getting highly talented individuals motivated and situated into a positive learning environment.

These case studies are provided from real situations. To provide privacy for the individuals involved in these case studies, the names have been changed.

So, roll up your sleeves and begin in the next section!

CASE STUDY 1: RAVI

Ravi (name changed) is 20 years old and has completed his undergraduate degree (Bachelor of Science in Mathematics) and currently is in the process of enrolling in Mumbai University for a Master's in Mathematics. He qualified for the Kishore Vaigyanik Protsahan Yojana (KVPY) program in 2012-13, an Indian program for mentoring and scholarships in basic sciences. He completed six levels in French (A, B and C, and all levels and B2 DEP-Commercial French from the *Alliance Francoise* in Mumbai). He also enrolled in music and is currently learning Carnatic music, a form of Indian classical devotional music.

The Case File

Early childhood. Hailing from an upper middle class family, his mother was able to give up her full-time job to support Ravi in his endeavors. Throughout, he took part in discussions and decisions related to his career and personal goals along with mentors and well-wishers.

Ravi's early milestones of development were delayed. He sat at eight months and walked with support when he was a year old. However, he exhibited curiosity when he was as young as four and a half months. Though he could not walk or move, he would roll to reach objects of interest. His mother reported that she realized he was different from other children when he was 1½ years old.

By 1½ years he showed a great interest for learning. He would try to examine switches, plugs, other electrical and engineering items and was proving dangerous. To keep him occupied, his mother bought a lot of books with pictures and read to him. By age two he was using a computer with his mother's assistance. His mother introduced him to new areas of interest and he started learning rapidly.

An ear infection awakens an early reading interest. He started play school when he was two years old because he was academically ready. But he disliked being away from his mother. By the time he was 4½ years old he had started school and he was able to read big encyclopedias.

His interest in the human body awakened when he developed a painful ear infection. Because of that, he had to avoid certain kinds of foods and wore a scarf to school, and several of his friends made fun of him for it.

When he asked his mother why he was suffering from ear pain she bought an encyclopedia of the human body to show him the parts of the ear to explain to him what was happening. It was this that awakened his interest. He first read about hearing—and then he went on to read the entire human body encyclopedia before he was five!

Ravi's gifted young family members. Ravi's cousin (his father's sister's daughter) has been identified as gifted and has been enrolled in a gifted children's program in Canada. His mother reported that this girl's younger brother was also a very sharp child, and that Ravi got along very well with him.

Ravi excelled in research and school by age eight. At seven to eight years of age, when he realized that his mother would refer to the Internet to explain many things for him, he started to also browse (supervised) to get more information on topics that interested him.

His thirst for knowledge, independent learning, and his deep resentment for rote learning, proved a challenge during his school days. He displayed advanced learning capabilities across subjects including languages. During his school days Ravi mastered his textbooks within a span of less than one month.

School did not excite him as he had already learned what was scheduled for the academic year.

As an eight-year-old in the third grade, he was rated first in his school's National Cyber Olympiad competition, and fourth in all of India in the National Science Olympiad event. He also appeared for the Maharashtra State Scholarship Exam, a exam for students from margianalized communities.

In the fourth grade, though, when Ravi questioned a science concept that was taught wrongly by the teacher, the teacher reprimanded him. And the corporal punishment he and other students were subjected to disturbed him. As a result, he withdrew into a shell.

Over the years of schooling, Ravi changed from the state board school system to a school with an Indian Certificate of Secondary Education (ICSE) curriculum, known for its comprehensive, rigorous, holistic approach to studies. He also enrolled in several online courses and competitions to keep himself busy.

One reason for the changes was that the ICSE school had a small class size of 20 to 25 students. Despite his mother's advice to not interrupt the class with questions, and reserve them for sessions after a class, Ravi was unable to contain himself. For example, when a teacher explained to the class that "The brain has four parts," Ravi interrupted and corrected her, saying, "The brain has ten parts." Other children were finding it difficult to understand even four parts to the brain, so the teacher found Ravi's interventions in class to be disruptive.

In those early school years Ravi was already interested in chemistry, particularly organic chemistry, because it is very systematic. He then discovered he wanted to specialize in cosmos chemistry. Copernicus, who specialized in several different fields, became his role model.

Similarly, Ravi had a wide range of interests, spanning math, history, geography, languages, etc. And he badly wanted to study abroad so he could simultaneously study subjects of science, math and languages together.

Moved to an IGCSE curriculum in the sixth grade. Ravi was moved to an International General Certificate of Secondary Education (IGCSE) program in the sixth grade because the ICSE program did not challenge him. The Indian IGCSE program is the equivalent to similar programs for bright students in the United Kingdom and the United States.

The program's pedagogic practices and respect for individual learning helped Ravi move ahead. While his knowledge in physics, chemistry, and biology was at a graduate level, his math level was only at eighth grade level. So his mother held him back in math so he would have at least one subject at school that would interest and encourage him to go to school.

It was while Ravi was in the eighth grade that the National Institute of Advanced Studies (NIAS) team visited Ravi in Mumbai. It was this first interaction with NIAS, a premier institute in Bengaluru that engages in interdisciplinary and multidisciplinary research in the arts, humanities, and the natural and social sciences that prompted Ravi's mother to visit the NIAS website, "Promoting and Developing India's Gifted Young" at www.prodigy.net.in and learned of other parents who faced similar issues.

Ravi's earliest concepts and inventions. Ravi kept a file of inventions and concepts he developed, such as a natural eco-friendly car; an air seat; an all-purpose gadget for cooking that combines options for cooking, microwaving, and grinding; and a techno-city, an eco-friendly city with hi-tech equipment. His detailed plans included administration, transportation, education, waste management, industry, security, and more, for the city.

His mother had written about this idea to Ratan Tata, a famous Indian industrialist and former chair of the Tata Group, who initially did respond asking for more details, but then communications stopped.

Ravi's mother also made attempts to contact leading organizations and institutions like Infosys and the Bhabha Atomic Research Center in Mumbai to find mentors for him. But Ravi was reluctant to share his ideas with others for fear they may steal his ideas.

Observations of Ravi's personality. Unlike children of his age, Ravi does not have many peers. He sits alone in school during his free time and works on formulas, or he ventures into a world of his imagination. He is a voracious reader and spends a considerable amount of time in libraries.

Observing his behavior, his fifth grade teachers had him take Institute for Psychological Testing standardized tests. He was found to have an IQ of 135. Only then did his mother realize that he was gifted, and she started reading up on the matter.

The entrance exams of Indian universities are largely based on the curriculum of the Central Board of Secondary Education (CBSE), a national board of education responsible for regulating the development of school education across India. Success in the Joint Entrance Exam (JEE) for certain universities depends largely on learning the CBSE curriculum.

Ravi has had an aversion to rote learning, so memorizing the CBSE curriculum and passing the JEE examination to gain adminssion to premier Indian institutes of technology was a great challenge for him.

Despite several conversations that the NIAS team held with Ravi to convince him to make the JEE leap, he refused; he could not be convinced.

Ravi pursues studies in science and is first rejected.
Instead, Ravi was keen to join the Indian Institute of Science
(IISc) in Bengaluru because he wanted to pursue pure science
rather than technology. Another reason for this choice was that
the NIAS and IISc are on the same campus, making it easier to
get mentoring support from both.

Ravi completed the 12th grade through the international
baccalaureate (IB) system with 39 points out of 45 and, on top
of that, he had to learn the additional subjects covered in the
CBSE curriculum. He lamented, "I felt I was disadvantaged as
I was handling two boards [IB and CBSE] at the same time."

However, admission to IISc required a certain rank on the
KVPY exam (page 182). He passed the exam and interview
and was awarded a scholarship but his rank fell short of the
cut-off for entry into the IISc's Indian Institute of Science Education and Research (IISER) program.

As an alternative, Ravi succeeded in one entrance test of a
university for a course in biotechnology, so he started attending
college.

"During the first semester," Ravi said, "I found that [instead
of] teaching the syllabus that was meant to 'bridge the gap
between students of different boards,' the teachers would skip
large portions of their syllabi saying that everyone had already
completed it because it was expected that a student from a CBSE
or ICSE board would have completed them. This included laboratory work of which I had very little experience. I was not given
any help nor was I allowed to practice independently in a lab in
the presence of a lab assistant. The teachers even became vin-
dictive and students distanced from me. This forced me to quit
college after the first semester."

An alternative to his first stumble and a second denial.
Because the biotechnology course was not considered a pure
science, he was told he was no longer entitled to the scholar-

ship. Disappointed, Ravi looked for an alternative to save his scholarship.

"As all admissions by then had closed, I joined a Bachelor of Science (B.Sc.) in Mathematics course by correspondence with Annamalai University, which was the only one that would make an exception and permit me to write the year-end exam at the end of the same academic year." *

Once enrolled in Annamalai Ravi again approached KVPY, with help from NIAS, to inform them that he had enrolled in their B.Sc. in Mathematics program, but the KVPY refused the scholarship on account that it was a "distance learning" course and not in person.

It was not scholarship money that was important to Ravi; it was that the program's rules favored or required a scholarship for access to the workshops and libraries he needed.

Mentoring advice to get back on track. Navi's NIAS advisors during several visits had told Ravi and his mother that a correspondence course in Bachelor of Science (B.Sc.) program would be of very little value in India—that he needed to get back to regular college as soon as possible.

They also recommended that Ravi seek opportunities to meet scholars in his area of interest and start corresponding with them, to follow their research work, and that he should attempt to write and publish in journals.

Taking their advice, Ravi approached a scientist in biochemistry, Ravi's field of interest then. She allowed him to participate in her research project despite being only 16 years old. But after only about a month of training in her lab she approached Ravi sadly with unwelcome news.

"The rules have changed," she told him, "and now only

---

* Students in Indian universities have to have a minimum of 75% attendance in the academic year to take the year-end exam. Ravi was short of this requirement as he had spent a few months enrolled in a biotechnology course.

students of the same university, and above the age of 18, are allowed to work on the research project."

This was bad news for him as he was then enrolled in the Annamalai University and not yet in the Indian Institute of Science (IISc).

Undeterred, Ravi continued his mathematics program at Annamalai University and informed his NIAS advisor that he had moved to Guruvayur, a small town in the Indian state of Kerala, while he completed the B.Sc. and continued French courses. His purpose was to study under a scholar of Indian philosophy and literature.

Meanwhile, IISc was organizing a conference on the subject of Science and Technology in Indic traditions.

Mentors guide Ravi to a new academic direction. Ravi's NIAS advisor saw the IISc conference on Indic traditions as a unique opportunity for Ravi, informed him about it and, although registration had closed by then, his advisor helped Ravi get registered and attend.

This event opened doors for Ravi as he was able to meet several scholars working in the Indic field of work that so intrigued him. The conference also led him to work on a research project with one of the professors based in Bengaluru (a city known as Bangalore until 2014), whom Ravi met at the conference.

Ravi next explored the possibility of relocating to Bengaluru to work with the Bengaluru professor, but Ravi's NIAS advisor recommended to Ravi that he instead enroll in a regular master's course in Mumbai (the Indian city formerly known as Bombay) which reflected his interests in auditing the courses of a professor with the top-ranking Indian Institute of Technology (IIT) in Mumbai, whom Ravi had also met at the IISc Indic conference and with whom he wanted to work and mentor. But Ravi had failed to impress the IIT Mumbai professor.

Seeing Ravi's disappointment, Ravi's NIAS advisor met with

him and said to Ravi the encouraging words he needed: "It's fine. Don't give up. Take a course with the professor and use that channel to reach the professor you want."

On the advice of his NIAS advisors, Ravi continued to follow the work of his potential professors and started attempts to publish in similar areas of study.

Meanwhile, the kind and understanding Bengaluru professor, with whom Ravi is working on a research project, also advised him to enroll in a regular master's course in Mumbai.

This trajectory has led Ravi to his current direction: to pursue a master of science (M.Sc. in Mathematics) at the Mumbai University; then a Master of Arts (MA in Sanskrit) by correspondence with the prestigious Rashtriya Sanskrit Sansthan Institute, an autonomous institution of the Indian Ministry of Educartion; and follow those two with a Doctor of Philosophy (PhD) to connect the two subjects.

His overarching plan is to undertake research in ancient Indian texts on mathematics.

Observations and Exercise

It is important to note that Ravi's interests, like many gifted children, will change trajectory; but it is the role of the mentor to connect the different interests and skill sets to advance toward the interest area chosen by the student.

The role of the mentor, or mentors, is crucial for Ravi and children like him in countries that do not have a formal education program for the gifted and talented. The experience of failure has to be converted into an opportunity while keeping the motivation of the student very high despite disappointments.

What is critical in this case study is the role of the mother, to be a constant mentor and support throughout the student's entire journey.

Finally, mentoring is an act that is shared in most cases

among several mentors. Each one has a unique contribution to the growth and development of the mentee.

Think back now about the previous chapters' discussions to see how they relate to this case study. What other observations can be made about Ravi's case using the "Keys to Effective Analysis" on page 180?

CASE STUDY 2: HARI

Hari (name changed) is currently in the 12th grade in a leading public school in Bengaluru, India. Access to both the ICSE and CBSE curriculums gave him an opportunity to engage in learning more meaningfully. He came to NIAS' attention in early 2013 when he was 13 years old. As a member of an upper middle class family, he has had the full support and the considerable resources of his parents and his extended family network.

The Case File

Early childhood. His early developmental milestones revealed that the child turned on one side after just three to four days of his birth, and he turned completely on his stomach when he was three months old. By his fifth month he was already crawling, and at eight months he was able to stand with help. Unlike normal children, he never sat but he started walking and by the age of 12 months he was able to walk independently.

Hari was precocious in language development. At just four months of age he first pointed to a light bulb and said, "light," and by the end of his fifth month, he had already developed an idiosyncratic vocabulary of 20 to 30 words with which he could communicate with caregivers. His receptive vocabulary—his ability to understand what was asked of him—was large, and he was able to speak simple sentences by the time he was one year old.

The child's early interests. At an early age of five or six years, Hari's father noticed his affinity for science-related books, his curiosity, and his demand for logical explanations. It was at this age that he started reading encyclopedias, and soon after, gradually, he started using computers to search for information.

At seven years of age he asked his father, "How fast do airplanes fly?"

Attempting to reply in an age-appropriate way, his father explained, "It is something like the speed of sound."

Immediately Hari countered, "But sound travels faster – if I speak to my grandfather on the phone I can hear him immediately; but if we visit him on the plane it takes much longer."

His father was pressed to explain that in the case of telephones sound is converted and transmitted as electrical impulses … and Hari grasped the concept. This showed his father that Hari, at that early age of seven, could reason, be critical, and relate observations from real life to learning.

Hari awakens to experimentations before age ten. There were several instances at an early age that Hari displayed interest in physics and a spirit of inquiry, becoming involved in spontaneous and independent experimentation.

For example, when he was about eight or nine he became interested in the behavior of water. In one occasion he used a pair of cylindrical toy magnets in the bathtub and noted that the magnets spun differently in water than they do in air. He kept spinning both magnets, which are designed to settle after motion at a set angle to each other. After several trials, he was able to understand that in water (in the bathtub) the magnets consistently ended up in a different alignment than when they were in air. And, as with other experiments, and as is typical for this age group, this experiment did not hold Hari's interest for long.

As he observed different things, Hari was also constantly thinking and asking, "What will happen?" and then conducted impromptu, unusual experiments, like freezing soap foam, or fermenting grape juice with yeast, as well as experiments that were explicitly forbidden, like heating deodorant bottles marked with the warning "Do not expose to heat." Although he was willing to "break the rules" he did so cautiously, and wore goggles for safety.

On another occasion, concerned with the depletion of non-renewable fuels, Hari got the idea of a world designed to minimize energy use and capture renewable energy. His idea centered on making vehicles less dependent on fuels. In this world, all roads would go downwards, with vehicles travelling using gravity; all roads would be undulating, and all destinations would be downhill from the start point.

In order to have all roads go downwards, vehicles and their occupants would first be hoisted to a high central point. In addition, while cars travelled down the roads, the energy of friction would be stored in batteries as supplementary fuel.

Though Hari's father later explained the flaw in this plan, Hari wondered if the renewable sources of energy such as solar energy could be harnessed to lift vehicles to the elevated point.

As a 12 to 13-year-old in seventh grade. In his quest to move away from the traditional curriculum, Hari started reading science fiction. When he was in the seventh grade, he was keenly interested in particle physics and string theory, and was consumed by the idea of time travel. He said, "We are free to move in all directions in space, but are helpless against the flow of time."

Hari made this observation when he was enrolled in a study center founded by Dr. B. S. Ramachandra, a renowned Indian scientist, polymath, author, and mentor for bright minds (known as "talent whisperer") with whom Hari shared a mutual interest in string theory. Dr. Ramachandras' center was an environment where students were free to choose their field of study.

He also developed an interest in entrepreneurship during that time, and expressed that "being the master of my own fortune would be a far less painful experience than working under someone else, as my primary school experiences indicated." Hari then added, "A sense of thrill and pride in being my own boss drew me further towards that dream."

Observations of Hari's personality. Hari is a curious boy and prefers a hands-on approach to learning. He is keenly interested in novel things. Anything new gets his attention, even if it is outside his existing areas of interest.

Repetition tires Hari quickly, and he resists work like copying questions and answers from texts. Generally, he is not impressive when required to formally present school work, unless he enjoys the assignment—then he awakens and manifests excellent presentation skills.

When Hari was in third grade, his father gave him a book on how to make paper airplanes. After some practice he mastered the craft and he decided to start a business, or at least what he thought business meant. He modeled it on the method used by automakers: sell the product and charge customers for ongoing service and maintenance. He made paper planes and put them up on display. There were different models, and each was sold at a fixed price, but the interesting "twist" in his scheme was that he also offered to provide customers with "maintenance services" like "re-creasing" the airplanes after a certain number of flights. This was early evidence of his entrepreneurial character.

In another example, "achievement" in the usual sense, as by demonstrating "mastery" at something, does not motivate him. For Hari a meaningful achievement is the more tangible cue of a numerical high "mark" or grade; that is, he feels he achieves when he scores well in tests, particularly in subjects that are difficult for him, like math. In other words, he uses marks as a means of *measuring* his mastery of a topic.

While Hari has demonstrated interest in physics, mechanics, and electronics, he does not respond favorably to explicit attempts to interest him in other areas, and his interests must be spontaneous and intrinsic. He resists being told what to do, or schedules being made for him. Advisors' attempts at scheduling activities failed as he refused to stick to a predetermined routine.

Hari is popular with friends and has a sense of humor that adults and older teens enjoy. He gets along well with children from third to twelfth grades. He is able to converse well with adults too. His sense of humor is reported to be beyond his age.

Extraordinary abilities in languages and the arts. Hari's mastery over the English language and command of verse was acknowledged by an English teacher to be as good as that of the leading poets of the English language. This sparked in Hari an interest to write many poems, often very intense, that he has published in a blog. He has also contributed to the scripts of many school programs.

Music is another interest of Hari's. This can be traced back to when he was two years old, when his mother exposed him to Carnatic music, a form of classical Indian devotional music.

Early attempts to enroll him in *vocal* Carnatic classes were not fruitful but he was fascinated by the flute, popularly used for Carnatic music, and he learned it quickly by age seven.

In addition to undertaking formal Carnatic lessons, he con-verted a lot of popular western songs into Carnatic notation. His playing of both Carnatic as well as popular songs was well appreciated at inter-school competitions he participated in. He maintains a blog site dedicated to Carnatic notes for western songs. Now, he trains under a flautist and a vocalist to enhance his techniques.

Hari's curiosity and ability to see patterns also led him to read far beyond his age and to question fundamental beliefs. For example, he wondered why he should learn Hindi at school when it is spoken by a miniscule population of the world. Instead, he set out to teach himself Arabic through the Internet and was soon able to read and write the language. He then tried to find Arabic literature online and, finding none, turned his interest to Persian.

Finding Persian closer to Hindi, and correlating with history, he drew his own conclusions about how languages, such as Hindi, possibly developed over the years.

He also took a deep interest in the similarities between Indian mythology and Greek mythology, drawing several parallels between the two. To explain his findings he unabashedly mapped in detail the characters of the two systems with findings that often disagreed with existing published works by notable authorities in this subject.

Mentors and Hari deal with his self-doubts. Despite his strengths, Hari's feeling of isolation from his middle school years continued. He had lost confidence in his abilities and believed he wasn't good at anything. This was when he had his first encounter with the National Institute of Advanced Studies (NIAS).

When Hari came to the NIAS in 2014 he was first profiled, as all new students are. The process, in Hari's words, "put me at ease, helping me to come to terms with some of my inner conflicts, and was able to make me see myself in a much better light."

After that, many interaction sessions occurred between Hari and a variety of NIAS people of different walks: research students, entrepreneurs, engineers, educators, counsellors, and more.

Following one such action, the NIAS connected Hari to the Swaanand Foundation, an Indian organization dedicated to "nurturing gifted children."

Joining the NIAS was a refreshing change for Hari—to be in the company of open and less rigid people. Hari looked forward to his interactions with NIAS. When describing these interactions, Hari said, "Their approach and confidence in my abilities made me feel that I had a direction in life, and a goal to work towards. However, I still felt that I did not have the right channels to realize my goals in the manner I desired."

Hari shared with his advisor his state of mind and experience at NIAS this way:

> This was one of the most difficult periods of my life. NIAS assigned me a mentor, who was an undergraduate research student at IISc. However, I was still in a period of great confusion, alternating between believing in myself and losing hope completely.
>
> Consequently, I interacted very little with my mentor. At our rare meetings, I would often discuss study routines and how I could improve my grades. He was open about his successes and failures and I found these meetings comforting.
>
> Later I attended the Open Day at IISc [a sort of science exposition] with him. That was where I saw for the first time the working of a non-Newtonian fluid. I was stupefied to see that there exists a substance which remains soft and pliable when handled gently, but turns rock solid under impact. The automobile enthusiast in me saw a potential application for this magic substance: an new kind of automobile suspension.

His teachers recognized that while he was competent and able, he had problems that held him back from success, so in 2014 his parents met the NIAS team, concerned about his academic performance and the conflicts he was going through.

Following those meetings, Hari's advisor connected him with an emminent adolescent and child psychiatrist in Bengaluru, and the two clicked immediately. Hari felt the psychiatrist understood his problems and how Hari could overcome them. Hari's sessions with him were uplifting and he found it easier to cope with his conflicts. This greatly helped him improve his academic score in the tenth grade.

Hari's confidence is restored and he takes off. Also in the summer of 2014, Hari entered the Google Science Fair, where he presented his "non-Newtonian fluid suspension." It was an arduous project to work on. Although it did not receive an award, he was quite satisfied with having learned so much about the functioning of a crucial component of most automobiles.

Later on he entered another contest: the NIAS Maiya Prodigy Fellowship Program, "a platform for highly self-motivated adolescents to engage in projects that help them gain specialized knowledge and experience in their particular areas of interest."

After winning this prestigious award, Hari summarized with the following words his successful transition from self-doubt to a highly productive mind:

> Receiving the NIAS-Maiya award was a landmark moment for me. It not only boosted my own confidence, but also made my peers and teachers believe in my abilities. Although I still relapse into moments of self-doubt, I am able to recover effectively when I relive my past successes, much of it due to the mentoring support I received at NIAS.
>
> Today, I find myself positively engaged with my school again and fascinated with subjects ranging from biomechanics to microelectronics and nanotechnology. My dream is to work in a technically advanced field which not only excites me, but can also impact fundamentally the way people live, work and travel. I can now recognize interesting topics within subjects that I did not pay too much attention to in the past. I am sure my future lies in the field of innovation; helping advance the state of art and practice in the field of technology.

Observations and Exercise

Hari's case study demonstrates the oscillations between self-doubt and discovery, accompanied with delight, that gifted and talented children experience. There is one subset of gifted children who often feel doubtful of their ability. The role of the mentor for these children is crucial, along with more frequent interaction to provide needed encouragement and reassurance for their very real talents.

Needless to say every gifted child is unique in some ways. Unless we analyze several case studies, it is difficult to understand their behavior patterns. Consequently, it is difficult to arrive at a common pattern of mentoring, as each one requires individual interventions that are unique to their circumstances and their personality.

For many of these children, the absence of a positive environment at home and school could be responsible for their expressed self-doubt and diffidence.

Think back now about the previous chapters' discussions to see how they relate to this case study. What other observations can be made about Hari's case using the "Keys to Effective Analysis" on page 180?

■ ■ ■

KEY POINTS ABOUT CASE STUDIES

This chapter examines two case studies that highlight the points of discussion in preceding chapters. Following are key points to note about why case studies are an important learning and teaching component for mentoring programs:

1. As a mentor, assume the role of a trusted friend; but when analyzing a mentee's profile and history, assume the role of a *detective* in search of activities' outcomes and causal information so program corrections can be made, if necessary, and effective methods are continued.

2. Document mentees' programs and progress, from intended plans of action to after action results; and apply the "Keys to Effective Analysis" to these records so mentors learn and adjust methods as mentees reveal themselves and evolve

through their programs.

3. Case studies are essential tools for learning and evaluations. They help synthesize critical, historical information that shows mentees' progress, or the lack thereof, over time that can reveal patterns, problems, and successes.

4. The efficacy of mentoring programs depends on the ability of staff to discern what works and what does not; and those findings come from the interaction records mentors create for their own individual use, and for program-wide statistical analysis.

11

Next-Generation Mentoring

When we mentor future generations, we sow
the seeds of inspiration, resilience, and growth,
knowing that they will blossom and shape the
world in ways we cannot even imagine.

— Malala Yousafzai

W E ARE IN the Fourth Industrial Revolution and have already entered the new age of artificial intelligence. With the rise of artificial intelligence, we can expect the ubiquitous presence of AI and its impact to be seen in every area of our lives. Businesses will be looking for a workforce that is competent in many aspects of the applications of AI. Top dollars will go to those who have experience with AI in production, marketing, sales, and the development of a multitude of products.

Customers will expect and demand new customer experiences

such as those that have already been implemented through online shopping. The rise of the "metaverse" as our new three-dimensional virtual reality workplace, play space, and replacement for the local shopping malls, will become commonplace in advanced societies.

Knowledge and information management will be the new resource guiding businesses and influencing contributions to all organizations. Teams will no longer be ad hoc formations of those with subject matter expertise, but become refined teams in which the best individual expertise and individual characteristics are analyzed, assessed, and placed together to form the most effective, efficient, solution teams imaginable. Changes and transformations will occur in ever faster speeds.

The lines between traditional mentoring, teaching, training, coaching, and counseling will become even more blurred as electronic devices replace traditional relationships in these activities. To obtain more value in mentoring, the mentor-protégé relationship must be more clearly defined and separated from these other activities.

As we enter the age of *Mentoring Beyond AI* we must explore these relationships to see how new tools may change mentoring and enable us to develop relationships faster, focus on transferring experiences more efficiently, and ultimately enable both mentor and protégé to gain maximum benefits out of the relationship in a world which more and more pressures us and limits our precious time.

MENTORING TERMINOLOGY

The terms "teaching," "training," "coaching," "counseling," and "mentoring" are often used interchangeably. While similar, they describe distinct areas and activities to achieve specific results, all of which describe aspects of mentoring, but are not in and of themselves considered mentoring.

Teaching

Teaching is a process of education, whereby the teacher imparts new knowledge and skills, as well as concepts and rules to a learner, enabling them to use these newly acquired elements as tools in a continuing process of knowledge accumulation.

Teachers facilitate adaptation of the knowledge and skills and application across the wide variety of situations. The relationship between teacher and student is one of respect and trust in longer term knowledge development.

Training

Training provides a formal method of learning specific skill sets or knowledge with well-defined learning objectives, usually to meet a minimum accepted standard of performance.

The relationship between the trainer and trainee is also formal and usually limited. Once the skill is learned, the trainer is no longer needed. The trainee then performs the task or skill individually while improving mastery up to and through the "expert" level.

Coaching

Coaching extends training, building upon the training baseline while aiding in skill development by pointing out problem areas, and providing definite techniques and suggestions to improve performance. From the relational dimension, a coach enters our lives for a specific skill or skills development in limited areas with specific achievement goals.

Coaching can take multiple forms; however, the four most popular are: Socratic, Hands-on, Interventionist, and Guiding (Brefi). The Socratic coach challenges by asking probing questions to engage the participant in mentally evaluating, correcting

Figure 11.1. The canopy of mentoring

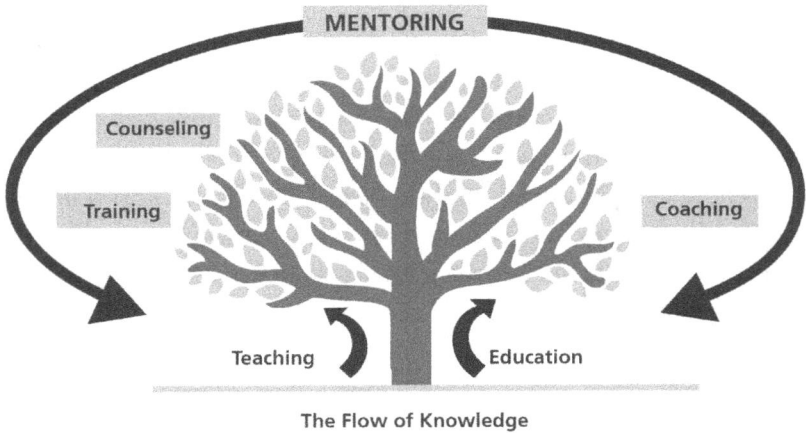

The Flow of Knowledge

and developing skills. Similarly, the hands-on coach will demonstrate specific skills and ways to improve or perform a task but leave it to the individual to develop specific techniques.

After participants have developed a basic skill level, coaching may shift to the interventionist methodology, where the coach observes activities and at key moments intervenes to help participants choose a specific path of action. A guiding coach will use the same methodology, to provide guidelines and boundaries within which the participant must remain. As the participants push the boundaries the guiding coach will nudge the participant back on course.

A guiding or intervening coach must be careful not to constrain the mentee in ways that truncate growth. Sidebar 11.1 on page 206 illustrates how one professor gently kept Bikramjit Basu, his doctorate mentee for enginering, ceramics-focused and on course through a difficult learning period while also encouraging the mentee to venture out of that known, familiar ground to explore and become expert in "tribology" and "biomaterials," new fields of work in which the mentee became expert.

Counseling

Counseling is another term which may be applied within the mentoring relationship, but is a highly skilled intervention focused on addressing identified, underlying psychological problems within the protégé (Brefi Group). Not all mentors are qualified to address psychological and behavioral problems which, once identified are better left for trained professionals. However, mentors must certainly be attuned to the psychological problems and provide advice and guidance on who may be able to help the protégé address these issues.

Mentoring

So, what is mentoring? Mentoring provides an overarching canopy of all of these areas, although mentoring is much more closely related to coaching (Figure 11.1). The primary difference, is the length of time and focus. Coaching is a short-term relationship based upon specific, focused skills necessary to accomplish the goal. Mentoring is a much longer term relationship, which could last a lifetime and is focused not just on those specific skill sets necessary to attain the goal but on broader skill sets necessary to integrate and enhance one's life.

Although mentoring skills can focus specifically in certain areas, such as academic achievement, the primary purpose is a much larger, holistic area focused on integrating a variety of skills sets to many focus areas.

A key characteristics of mentoring is its focus on an ongoing relationship that lasts over a long period of time. Mentoring can vary from very informal meetings to provide the protégé general advice, guidance, or support, to a more formal, professional relationship focused on more specific goals such as business, academics, or life skills.

To be effective, mentoring must focus on the long-term

Sidebar 11.1. Confinements of our own making

BIKRAMJIT BASU, PROFESSOR
Materials Research Center, Indian Institute of Science, Bengaluru, India

A mentor is the one who imparts knowledge and wisdom, aids in assimilating critical concepts and teaches moral values. Such was Omer, a professor at *Katholieke Universiteit Leuven* (KUL), Belgium and my mentor during my doctoral work in late last century.

Having received bachelor's and master's degrees in metallurgical engineering in India, I decided to do my doctoral studies in Belgium in the emerging field of engineering ceramics. This was unconventional as most Indian students during my time preferred to pursue such studies in the United States.

I arrived in Belgium on a cold day, and I was surprised to be received by my supervisor, Omer, at the airport. I appreciated his help settling in on the first day in a foreign land.

Soon after arriving I was offered a Nehru-Cambridge scholarship in England instead, but Omer convinced me to continue my Ph.D. course work at KUL. Tempting as it was, Omer's fine advice has helped me reach where I am today.

Despite my training in metallurgy, I never had any course on ceramics in India. Dedicated to his students, Omer tirelessly disseminated knowledge, and he clarified all my queries and doubts, including the most rudimentary questions in the field of engineering ceramics.

Upon learning the basics, Omer steered me to design and conduct experiments with sinter ceramics. As an undergraduate I knew ceramics are used as refractories in blast furnaces and basic oxygen furnaces to produce molten steel. But I never dreamt that I would pursue a career in this. As I read up I was amazed by ceramics, and hands-on training in ceramic processing helped me understand the theories. His way of mentoring was simply exciting and thought-provoking. He is undoubtedly the master in his domain of expertise.

Soon I progressed to conducting tribology experiments to determine performance limits. And, as in my initial days understanding the basics of ceramics, I had to learn tribology, an extremely new subject for me, but Omer motivated me to get familiar with the nitty-gritties of it. With his untiring support, I successfully learned the subject and designed and conducted experiments.

Omer's prodding to learn a completely new subject and excel in that domain indeed impacted my carrier as a researcher. Now I lead research in the interdisciplinary area of biomaterials science and engineering, renewable energy, and more.

Omer's mentoring went beyond science. Our discussions in his office late into the night showed me his extremely hard-working nature and his charismatic work culture that has permeated into my research work and teach-

benefits to the protégé and require the mentor to have a much broader view of the person and the protégé's characteristics.

In most mentor-protégé relationships, the mentor is often a senior person with more experience, expertise or higher qualifications than the protégé. But experience, expertise and higher qualifications or not the only keys to success in the mentor-protégé relationship. The mentor must be able to transfer their experience or expertise to the protégé while at the same time broadening the protégés' outlooks, values, and beliefs and opening doors for them to discover new, previously out of reach opportunities, as Figure 11.1 on page 204 illustrates. While the focus on mentoring is usually on career and personal development, the mentor must provide a broad, strategic framework upon which the protégé can construct their own future.

MENTORING TYPOLOGIES

In the most basic sense, mentoring can be categorized in several contrasting ways, such as formal-informal mentoring, traditional-reverse mentoring, and passive-active mentoring.

In a formal mentoring relationship, interactions are highly structured and institutionalized. In many cases these relationships

Confinements of our own making (continued)

ings. He also sponsored a number of my trips to Spain, the United Kingdom, Holland, and Luxembourg to attend scientific events. During such trips, he taught me how to interact with international researchers in diverse cultures—experiences that gave me an invaluable global perspective.

Learning from Omer to explore unfamiliar waters later on gave me the confidence to venture into the unknown domain of "biomaterials." We have to cross the boundaries of different disciplines to push out of one's own comfort zone to realize something new in life. I firmly believe that if one is clear in one's knowledge and thoughts in one core domain (materials science, for me), one should be able to intelligently adapt to explore new horizons, even without a formal training in that "new" area.

are focused on the organizational needs using assigned mentors with measurable outcomes and in a fixed duration, focused mentoring role.

Informal mentoring on the other hand, develops from informal, voluntary and loosely structured personal relationships. Rather than being organizationally directed, these relationships often evolve naturally as people seek advice from others with common interests. As informal networks grow, protégés are much more likely to encounter mentors willing and able to assist them through an informal mentoring relationship based upon the protégés needs and the mentor's skills and experience. Informal mentoring relationships are more likely to be open in duration, ranging from an immediate, situational mentoring relationship to one that may last a lifetime (Ohio).

Traditional-Reverse Mentoring

These relationships are defined by the age or experience of the mentor and protégé. In traditional mentoring, the mentor is one who has more experience, usually based upon age and is willing to take a protégé under wing in order to share their acquired knowledge in helping the protégé meet educational or career goals.

Reverse mentoring describes the relationship where senior protégés are assigned to or select younger mentors who can provide expertise in areas where the younger mentor may have more wisdom or a different perspective. Apple CEO Steve Jobs may have had this in mind when he quipped to CNBC,

> It doesn't make sense to hire smart people and then tell them what to do; we hire smart people so they can tell us what to do.

Reverse mentoring enables smart, experienced protégés to tap into another generation's insight to bridge generational gaps, obtain significant new or different insights, and "connect with younger, newer, or less experienced workers within an organization" (Ohio) to enhance organizational engagement and commitment. Perhaps more importantly, it provides a way for more senior mentors to "retool" and change careers.

Passive-Active Mentoring

Relationships defined by the role of the mentor are known as passive-active mentoring and requires no special work from the mentor. The mentor meets with the protégé on an established basis, but does not prepare or actively assist in developing the relationship beyond what was initially defined either by the organization or by agreement with the protégé.

Passive mentoring enables the protégé to take the lead in discussions, principally using the mentor as a sounding board for ideas. Passive mentoring provides a protégé with an admirable role model who provides inspiration, wisdom or insight by their example, and encouraging words. In some cases, a passive mentor may not even know they are providing mentorship to a protégé (ibid).

Active mentoring, on the other hand is a relationship in which the active mentor takes an interest in and knows the protégé. The active mentor uses his knowledge to continuously build and refine the mentor-protégé relationship. By doing so, the mentor develops agility in the wide range of mentoring activities and techniques, anticipating and providing the needed mentoring to the protégé. While many mentoring situations begin with active mentoring, over time these relationships fade into a passive mentoring profile.

Researchers in the U.K. developed a research program to evaluate the development of mentoring programs by identifying the typology of these two foregoing mentoring applications (Busse). Within the protocol, researchers developed a framework matrix to compare cases with categories derived from analysis obtained in audiotaped personal interviews using a mentoring program topic guide to delve into the specifics of the mentoring programs in order to develop a typology.

In 28 mentoring programs studied investigators developed three overarching categories based upon 1) the mentoring program's overall aim, 2) the target group, and 3) the type of mentoring program setting. Each of the three categories was further broken down into a range of subcategories. Based upon these subcategories, researchers identified 12 "mentoring models" which could be broadly grouped into two main models; personal and developmental and educational and employability models (ibid).

These characteristics match the traditional mentoring methodologies from the time of *Odysseus* and Mentor and employ traditional tactics, techniques and procedures to obtain the results, despite their application in the modern world.

So, what can we expect from the next generation of mentoring? Next, we begin to peek into the future.

Next Generation Mentoring

Next generation mentoring is where we go from the present to the future. The terms and definitions we use have evolved over time, and our twelve types of mentoring applications, mentoring terminology, tactics, and techniques primarily describe a traditional relationship between the mentor and protégé. Why? In past years, life moved at a much slower pace where the expectations were that a mentee would spend significant time with the mentor developing the necessary strategic infrastructure for their success.

In many cases the protégé could be expected to spend several years of their life as a disciple of the mentor, slowly learning and absorbing the necessary information. The traditional mentor protégé relationship has also been one in which a somewhat more mature and intelligent mentor worked with average or slightly above average intelligence protégés.

Historically, relationships between mentors and extremely gifted protégés have been limited in their success, as the protégés have quickly exceeded the capacity of their mentors to mentor.

Gifted mentors often do not have the patience or personal skills to develop the full relationships necessary for mentoring other gifted mentors. In many cases this has been due to the limits of their own mentoring, which has often been restricted by traditional mentoring methodologies.

Let's now examine what future mentoring will likely look like.

ACTIVE MENTORS OR ACTIVE MENTORING?

In 2010, Ron Nash published his book *Active Mentor: Practical Strategies for Supporting New Teachers*, a resource demonstrating "how to build active teacher mentoring programs that foster teacher retention and increase the effectiveness of new teachers."

Using the principles of the active classroom to engage students for higher achievement, Nash outlined several strategies for increasing and promoting professional development for teachers emphasizing the importance of creating a schoolwide climate for mentoring, and illustrating the critical role of mentors in providing teacher support (Nash). His concepts have been incorporated in a variety of educational settings since that time, all focusing on the active mentor as previously defined in active mentoring.

Although the traditional "educational and employability" model remains a mentoring mainstay, these questions arise for the future: "How can we mentor more efficiently, effectively and faster in the 21st century?" and, "Have we begun addressing the necessary changes in our mentoring models to meet our changing needs for the next generation of mentoring, or will we continue to use our traditional mentoring methodologies?"

The questions today's generation must address as we look to next generation mentoring are:

What does active mentoring mean today? Active mentoring requires more than just an active mentor understanding the protégé, and taking actions to continuously build and refine the mentor-protégé relationship. Today, the mentor must be able to develop and use a broader set of tools as well as agility in the wide range of mentoring activities and techniques to provide the needed mentorship for the protégé. This must also be an active process with the protégé taking actions to assist the mentor in developing agility and flexibility in the relationship. To do this, both mentor and protégé must actively seek the use of emerging technologies as active mentoring is about communications.

[The] traditional "educational and employability" model remains a mentoring mainstay,… [but we] can … mentor more efficiently, effectively and faster in the 21st century ... [by leveraging] new methods of communicating through social media and electronic devices.

We have already discussed communications in Chapter "3", including new methods of communicating through social media and electronic devices. Mentors employing active mentoring learned to use all available communication media to effectively reach and communicate with today's protégés. Relationships can be effectively maintained by using text messaging, video calls, or other social media platforms in addition to face-to-face communications.

The key is that the relationship maintain meaningful dialogue using all forms of communication to enhance the mentor–protégé relationship. Technology is an enabler. Leverage it seeking new and interesting ways to maintain the mentoring relationship. Be creative but not intrusive.

What is the state of active mentoring implementation plans across our programs? Having a plan for mentoring is quite different from implementing active mentoring. The key element in this equation is active. Active mentoring begins with active listening—knowing what the protégé wants in the relationship and delivering it.

Senior program personnel must constantly be reviewing mentoring plans and including new ways to improve implementation. If nothing else, our experience with Covid-19 and the requirement to work remotely identified that we are in a time of incredible change. Disruption of both our personal and professional lives led to increased loneliness and separation from our support systems. Active mentorship provides a means of bridging the gap. The use of corporate resources in innovative ways such as allowing video conferencing for communications in the mentoring program can go a long way in maintain the relationships.

What are the benefits of active mentoring? Active mentoring can help accelerate the mentoring process, while simultaneously developing a deeper, richer mentor-protégé relationship. Through this deeper richer relationship, the protégé will be able to feel free to express their needs and goals and the mentoring relationship, thus taking more ownership of the mentoring process and mentoring outcomes.

What are the most challenging areas in establishing an active mentoring environment? In today's ultra high-speed world with everyone constantly multitasking, mentoring can be a real challenge when either the mentor or mentee want to meet more frequently. Maintaining an aggressive meeting schedule may prove to be impossible. It is important to establish the program guidelines and a recommended meeting schedule from the outset. Incorporation of technology may lead to an ability to squeeze more time into an already busy schedule.

It is important that meeting schedules between the mentor and protégé be maintained. Disruptions in the schedule, including frequent postponements may lead to an erosion of the mentoring relationship. Make sure both the mentor and mentee prioritize time for the meetings. Mentoring is an important priority activity and should not be thought of as an extracurricular activity. Maintain accountability for the meetings and meet as scheduled.

Another element that must be taken into account at the outset of the program is expectations. Either the mentor or the protégé can have unrealistic expectations that would negatively impact the relationship. For example, the mentor may expect the mentee to have similar learning capabilities and experiences in which the mentor may overwhelm the mentee with information. Conversely, a mentee may be expecting unrealistic support and direction from the mentor. It is important to set the mentoring objectives and goals at the beginning of the program, and reevaluate and refine those expectations as the relationship develops.

Overdependence is another challenge in the mentoring relationship. The mentor must focus on the protégé's needs, which includes offering information and support while letting the protégé find their own path. Mentees may also come to rely heavily on their mentor's approval, rather than making their own decisions without fear of criticism. The mentor protégé relationship should encourage independence. This requires that mentors always remember that the relationship is about the mentee, while protégés value their mentors as one of many sources of information and support, not the only source of information and support.

What actions can mentor's take for active mentoring success? Researchers such as Kraiger et al have identified a variety of actions or enactments that provide "specific, nuanced" elements for mentoring success. The following items provide a quick look at some enactments, adapted from the "Cuboid of Mentoring" developed by Kraiger et al, which can be used to enhance mentoring:

1. **Build personal relationships** by exploring long-term goals of the protégé and reinforce to the protégé that they can discuss anything at any time either good or bad, with their mentor.
2. **Instill accountability while building confidence**. It is important that the protégé understand the importance of clearly developing the message the protégé wants to convey to others and consistently building confidence promoting adaptability conveying their message and meeting their goals.
3. **Improve confidence and competence**. The mentor can actively seek out areas, projects and opportunities for the protégé to improve their competence in particular skill sets. In addition, introduction of the mentee to additional people will help them build their professional network provide additional resources for the mentee.

Are the mentoring styles and typologies derived from traditional mentoring providing us appropriate methodologies for future mentoring? Although mentoring styles have been around since the beginning of the Greek idea of mentoring, it is important that mentors analyze their methodologies, adapt and learn new techniques, and implement new methods for mentoring that are effective for today's multicultural protégés.

Mentors should constantly be reviewing the literature and advances in mentoring, while appropriating and adapting new techniques. Some methodologies will remain tried-and-true. But only the mentor can assess the learning approaches and most effective methodologies for their protégés.

■ ■ ■

KEY POINTS ABOUT NEXT-GENERATION MENTORING

In this chapter we defined traditional mentoring typologies and introduced what may be the future of mentoring: active mentoring or mentors. Some key points about next-generation mentoring follow:

1. Although distinct from these activities, mentoring provides an overarching canopy for other activities such as counseling, training, coaching, and teaching.

2. A mentor must provide a broad, strategic framework upon which the protégé can construct their own future.

3. Informal mentoring experiences include; traditional-reverse mentoring relationships defined by age or experience, passive-active mentoring defined by the role of the mentor, and next generation mentoring.

4. Active mentors and active mentoring are more than just terms and require adaptation of emerging technologies and communication techniques.

5. Mentors must actively analyze their methodologies adapt, and learn new techniques, and implement new methods for mentoring that are effective for today's international, multicultural protégés.

12

Mentoring Gifted
Protégés

Mentoring gifted protégés requires recognizing and
valuing their strengths while also challenging them
to push beyond their comfort zones.

—Sally M. Reis

SUCCESSFUL MENTORING REQUIRES commitment
and diligence by the mentor. This is even more important
in the case of mentors mentoring gifted protégés. This requires
mentors to use active mentoring techniques, and as well have
powerful toolkits available for engaging the protégé, developing
the relationship, and providing counseling when and if needed
at a very early stage.

The following case study is a composite of some very interesting mentoring which proved less than successful due to late interventions by the mentors.

CASE STUDY 3: STAN

Stan was a brilliant computer science graduate student from one of the top universities in the United States. As a gifted student, Stan had no problems with his classwork, even at the highest levels.

In fact despite the challenge of attending one of the top universities, and taking classes under other, gifted professors and researchers, Stan was only marginally challenged. His capacity for having a near photographic memory and nearly perfect recall enabled him to advance rapidly through his coursework.

While completing his doctoral studies, Stan focused on an emerging area of research, where he quickly developed scientific breakthroughs and national renown.

Upon graduation, he sought a position in a major public research university where he was expected to perform equally in the three areas of teaching, research, and community service.

The Case File

Stan leverages doctoral student success to a professorship. Stan was recruited by several preeminent public research universities in which he hoped to focus principally in his emerging area of research, and for which the universities were actively recruiting him. Stan selected a large, but less established regional university with a large number of minority, underrepresented, and international students, many of which were the first generation to attend college in their families.

After accepting the university's offer, Stan visited the area searching for a house. While working with his realtor, Stan was unable to find acceptable housing within the financial range he thought he should be paying, and within a comfortable distance to the university and the city's main attractions.

Following several months of searching, the realtor was able

to narrow the available housing to five condominiums that met Stan's stated criteria.

Observations of Stan's personality. As the realtor and Stan visited each of the houses to make a final selection, Stan became more and more irritable, began changing his housing criteria, and after visiting the last house on the list, Stan appeared to have a breakdown.

He screamed at the realtor, "I can't make a decision under this intense pressure," then sat down in the middle of the floor and began rocking back and forth … murmuring to himself.

After about an hour, he calmly got up, told the realtor, "I'll get back to you," and left the condominium.

Some days later, he called the realtor and coldly stated that he had made a decision and would like to enter a contract for one of the houses.

The realtor, who knew some of the university administrators, mentioned the unusual behavior to the administrators.

Before and after Stan's departure, many of the faculty and staff that worked with him commented on his sharp eye for detail and perfection in getting facts. Every typographical error on a slide presentation was quickly identified by Stan and the issue became less about the topic being discussed and more about the perfection of the presentations. This was also true for written documents Stan received.

Stan's perfectionist tendencies also moved into the classroom, where several of his students had dropped his course, stating that "Professor Stan was too much of a perfectionist" and they could not meet his high expectations.

Stan's university mentors' passive approach. At the university, the department chair was finalizing his decision on who would be the best faculty mentor to assign to this new associate professor.

Figure 12.1. Gifted protégés present extraordinary challenges

TALENT MANAGEMENT

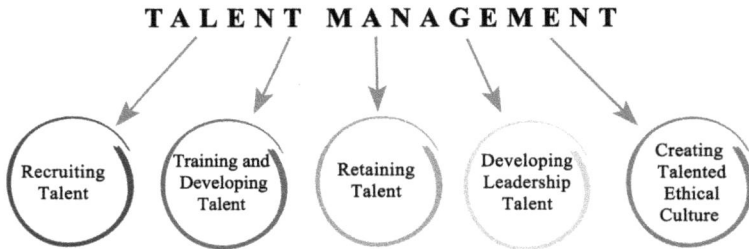

| Recruiting Talent | Training and Developing Talent | Retaining Talent | Developing Leadership Talent | Creating Talented Ethical Culture |

Source: Dmitry/stock.adobe.com

The university had recently established a policy of organizational mentoring to provide a "quick start" for new professors entering the field. He selected one of his top, most experienced professors to become Stan's mentor.

Professor Pam was a no-nonsense professor, and expert in her research field, who had been at the university for many years. She knew the ins and outs of the university and the many pitfalls of academia that could quickly trip up new professors trying to establish a name for themselves.

Upon being assigned as Stan's mentor, she obtained some background on Stan, then contacted him to establish their mentoring schedule and to get to know one another. Stan was aloof to the mentoring proposal and appeared to be somewhat disinterested to work with the senior professor. Although polite, he attended only one meeting with her, and then began conducting all of his interactions through email.

Sensing that Stan would prefer not to be mentored, Professor Pam reported back to the department chair, stating that she had met with the new professor and that he seemed to prefer to work his way into the university on his own. Knowing that he was a brilliant young man, and had come from a renowned university, and was very much absorbed by his ongoing research, both Professor Pam and the department chair elected not to pursue active mentoring.

During the first semester, Stan displayed enthusiasm for teaching and his research, and submitted several new academic classes to be included into the curriculum, which he would teach.

His second semester also seemed to go well as he enthusiastically began teaching these new courses and continuing to teach a few of the university's core curriculum courses. During this time, he also attended several research conferences and submitted multiple research papers and research funding proposals.

Unmanaged disappointments and perfectionism. As he continued his research and sought out new research conferences, he began to feel extremely constrained by his teaching schedule, and unable to attend what he considered to be several key research conferences. More importantly, he could not understand why his students could not understand the "basic concepts" he presented in class.

At the start of the fall semester in his second year, Stan discovered that many of his recent peer-reviewed articles had been rejected by the major conferences in which his work had previously been accepted. Additionally, research proposals Stan had submitted to advance his research were continuing to be rejected.

A gifted protégé fails and quits. At the end of this second fall semester, Stan resigned from his position at the university declaring that his principal reason for leaving was that "I really don't like teaching."

Within 18 months of beginning his university professorship, this new shining star had imploded.

Observations and Exercise

Could a better, more aggressive active mentoring program have saved Stan's career? We can only guess.

We do, however, have some indicators of areas where

interaction—or intervention—may have been useful, or necessary. Was Stan's perfectionism, as students and faculty observed, just a case of a professor setting the academic achievement bar too high? Or was there a behavioral problem in which Professor Stan just failed to adapt to the reality of dealing with students who were not as gifted as he was? In light of these indicators and Stan's known breakdown with his realtor, did Stan have a behavioral issue that needed to be addressed but was not?

What could the department chair, Professor Pam, or others, have done early on to guide their bright, young professor to better cope with the requirements of his new career?

Could cross-age mentoring have been a useful method for developing Stan as a gifted mentor? (See "Cross-Age Mentoring" on page 224.)

Looking at Figure 12.1 on page 220, did the university seem to follow an effective talent/mentoring management program? They did effectively recruit talent, but were they short in training, developing leadership, and adapting the new professor into his new culture? They cerrtainly failed in retaining their shining new star.

Perhaps a stronger, more active mentoring program would have been beneficial for Professor Stan and saved Stan's career. More importantly, had the university devoted time to developing gifted mentors for their gifted faculty members, could things have been different?

We think so.

Think now about the previous chapters' discussions to see how they relate to this case study. What other observations can be made about Stan's case using the "Keys to Effective Analysis" on page 180?

DEVELOPING GIFTED MENTORS

Developing leadership and mentoring skills in gifted protégés has previously not been given high priority in many gifted and talented programs (CNBC; Nash). And researchers such as Walter Gonsoulin and Sandra Manning have indicated that gifted youths, who themselves serve as mentors, can *gain* the experience and skills necessary to lead and mentor others.

Non-Traditional Mentoring

Mentors of gifted protégés should seek opportunities outside of the traditional mentoring program or relationship in which these gifted students can be immersed in real-world experiences which expose them to various situations. Through these encounters working with and leading others, gifted students can see the results of their work with others while practicing their leadership skills.

"Cross-age mentoring" is a form of near peer mentoring, where a [gifted student] is … [paired with a mentee] closely related in age.… under the guidance of [a] mentor where they can fully explore their actions and develop their leadership potential.

This model provides participating mentors with the opportunity to "acquire lifelong leadership skills and develop a greater commitment to community and stewardship." (Besnoy)

It is important for mentors to also provide opportunities for these gifted students to critique their own successes and failures under the guidance of the mentor where they can fully explore their actions and develop their leadership potential (Besnoy; Grassinger et al).

Cross-Age Mentoring

"Cross-age mentoring" is a form of near peer mentoring, where a mentor is selected from a group of protégés closely related in age. For example, using first or second year university students to mentor high school students who are about to enter the universities themselves, or high school students mentoring middle school or elementary school students.

This model provides participating mentors with the opportunity to "acquire lifelong leadership skills and develop a greater commitment to community and stewardship." (Besnoy) This type of mentoring can provide excellent opportunities for developing gifted mentors.

Mentors and their protégés will often need to be better matched to meet the goals and expectations of the program. This is especially important in the case of more gifted protégés.

■ ■ ■

KEY POINTS ABOUT GIFTED PROTÉGÉS

Mentoring gifted protégés presents extraordinary challenges to mentors and administrators of mentoring programs. Thus, gifted protégés may well require advanced methods to recruite them and, as importantly, to retain and develop them to their full potential. Following are key points about mentoring gifted protégés:

1. Development of gifted protégés requires mentors who have been trained and understand gifted students and are equipped to develop their extraordinary skills.

2. "Cross age mentoring," a form of near-peer mentoring, is a highly effective method of mentoring which could be applied to mentoring gifted protégés.

C H A P T E R

13

Advanced Technology and New Challenges

*When we long for life without difficulties, remind
us that oaks grow strong in contrary winds and
diamonds are made under pressure.*

— Peter Marshall

NOWADAYS, THE ENTIRE world can be thought of as a single global village, with interactions taking place simultaneously across the globe. Yet mentoring has remained a local activity. Despite our emphasis on multicultural understanding, global markets and international relations, we've been unable to develop mentoring as a global concept. The NIAS Maiya Prodigy Talent Search program (Maiya) was established as an important step to break these international and cultural barriers and allow students to be mentored by a group of international experts.

This concept provides for a multicultural experience, which will accelerate the protégés' capacity to perform in the international arena. The program seeks experienced international mentors who have traveled extensively gaining their experiences by having lived and worked in cultures across the globe.

New international mentoring initiatives will need to recruit and capitalize on the multicultural international experiences of their mentors. As always, technology will play a critical role in the development of these mentors and their ability to assist their protégés in understanding our complex but highly interconnected international communities.

The future of next-generation mentoring will depend upon two key elements—the experiences, willingness, and technological abilities of multicultural mentors to mentor the global village, and the availability of advanced technologies for these mentors to expand their expertise, while smoothly, flexibly, and adroitly communicating and interacting with their protégés.

As we enter the new age of AI, it has already become evident that AI and other technologies will be a ubiquitous presence in all aspects of our lives, driving our interactions, relationships, and mentoring in the future.

UNDERSTANDING ARTIFICIAL INTELLIGENCE

How intelligent is artificial intelligence? What do concurrent artificial intelligence programs and tools do and when do we know they have failed? Are artificial intelligence programs really humanlike? Do we expect them to become more humanlike in the future? Ultimately, will human mentoring be replaced by AI with "human-level" intelligence?

These are all questions that scientists, scholars, and citizens have been grappling with for decades but with the advent of modern technology catapulting us into the AI Age, it has never been more important for us to answer these questions. To answer these questions, we must better understand AI.

[T]he potential for misuse of AI technology as well as the potential for bias and unreliability, and its vulnerability to cyber-attacks are legitimate concerns. However, … "humans tend to overestimate AI advances and underestimate the complexity of our own intelligence."

In her book, *Artificial Intelligence, a Guide for Thinking Humans*, Melanie Mitchell provides an excellent overview of AI's past, present, and future. As a former student of Douglas Hofstadter, a cognitive scientist and Pulitzer prize-winning author, she explains why he is "terrified" about the future of AI. And she explores the profound disconnect between AI hype and AI's actual achievements. Recent hype concerning AI has raised the fear that AI has already become conscious, can turn malevolent, and could ultimately enslave or kill us (277). Granted, the potential for misuse of AI technology as well as the potential for bias and unreliability, and its vulnerability to cyber-attacks are legitimate concerns. However, Mitchell's bottom line is that worries about AI are "decidedly premature" and that "humans tend to overestimate AI advances and underestimate the complexity of our own intelligence" (278).

Traditional AI

So, what is AI anyway? Britannica defines artificial intelligence as, "the ability of a digital computer or computer-controlled robot to perform tasks commonly associated with intelligent beings" (Britannica). Here's where the definition gets a little sticky. What are *intelligent beings*? Intelligent beings represent multiple combinations of diverse abilities, including the ability to learn, reason, solve complex problems, perceive the environment around them, and to quickly adapt to change. While computers have been programmed to carry out very complex tasks, scientists have not been able to advance AI sufficiently to match human capabilities in melding these traits.

AI researchers employ methods to reach one of three goals in creating AI systems:

Artificial general intelligence machines built to *think*. This was the early goal of artificial intelligence and the main concept that the general population thinks of when they hear the expression "AI." This is also the area in which advances have been so meager that other AI technologists have felt that it is no longer "worth pursuing" (ibid).

Applied AI aims to produce commercially viable "smart systems" (ibid). This branch of AI has mostly been applied to information processing and has seen the most expansion and growth in the past few years.

Cognitive simulation on the other hand uses computers to test theories about the human mind and has become a powerful tool in both neuroscience and cognitive psychology (ibid).

These first forms of AI can be considered traditional AI. They focus on "performing a specific task intelligently" (Marr). This type is capable of extracting connections or "learning" from data to make decisions or predictions based on that data.

Readers are probably most familiar with these traditional types of AI in the form of Siri or Alexa. In these systems, they have been trained to follow specific rules to retrieve information or perform tasks; however there is no "thinking" to create new activities, systems, or information.

The Newer Generative AI

Generative AI is another form of AI that is gaining significant press recently. In generative AI, the system uses its learned data to create new images, information, and text, based upon a user's input. Essentially, it is copying its previously learned styles and patterns to generate new information that mirrors its original training set of data.

OpenAI's ChatGPT and it's more advanced GPT-4 represent the most current versions of Generative Pre-Trained Transformers (GPT) technologies in natural language processing.

ARTIFICIAL INTELLIGENCE AND DEEP LEARNING

Researchers from Google's DeepMind Team recently incorporated artificial intelligence in their program AlphaGo to develop the first program to defeat a world champion in the ancient game of Go. The program uses deep neural networks to evaluate positions and select moves in the game, gaining superhuman proficiency.

The neural networks were trained by supervised machine learning* from human expert moves, as well as incorporating reinforcement machine learning† from self-play. Most recently,

---

* Supervised machine learning allows a software program to be developed by providing both input and desired output data, or "examples" that the computer can use to infer the correct function. Thus the "supervisor" provides the desired outcome or answer which is used to correct the algorithm. In human psychology, this is referred to as "concept learning."

† Reinforcement machine learning, unlike supervised learning, does not provide the answer. Instead, the software must collect training examples through trial and error in an attempt to maximize the long-term reward.

the team developed AlphaGo Zero—a game changer and artificial intelligence and deep learning.

Their new system uses deep neural networks with parameters representing the board position, its history, and outputs of move probabilities and uses them in games of self-play to train the program. Using this self-play reinforcement learning concept alone, AlphaGo Zero without any supervision or use of human data, "learned" the game of Go and was able to develop super-human performance, winning 100 to 0 against the previous AlphaGo programs, which had themselves defeated the world's champion Go players.

This is an amazing feat in and of itself. However, the program was able to develop new strategies for winning the game that had not been employed in the more than 3000-year history of the game. It had truly "learned" something new!

Synthesizable AI for Mentoring?

Researchers at Florida International University (FIU) are working with a research team at Louisiana State University (LSU) who have developed an artificial intelligence known as "Synthesizable Artificial Intelligence," or SAI, which provides a unique dimension to artificial intelligence and deep learning.

Traditionally, artificial intelligence systems such as AlphaGo remain in a single dimension or domain. AlphaGo's domain is learning and playing the game of Go. SAI enables programs to work across domains to apply the learning in new, previously unexplored dimensions. This more closely resembles how humans can learn new concepts and apply them in completely different areas to achieve results and develop new knowledge.

The FIU research team is now exploring the potential for using SAI and other deep learning to develop new strategies and methodologies across domains, using virtual reality so that humans can see the resulting changes. This could enable reverse engineering of the deep learning processes to develop appropriate human learning, faster and more completely than can currently be comprehended by humans.

Could we apply the same concepts to expand mentoring methodologies, enabling both mentors and protégés to develop their skills far faster than current mentoring methodologies allow? Could these then be incorporated into modern E-Learning and E-Mentoring technologies? Would these new methods enable us to develop deeper human relationships in the mentoring process?

We think so. Answers to these questions may provide us with the next great leap for next-generation mentoring.

Innovations in Digital Mentoring Tools

The use of innovative technological tools is becoming more and more essential to the mentoring process as a means of allowing mentors, as well as protégés to do more in the time they have available. Digital devices have accelerated our pace of life and have become embedded as essential communication, educational, and entertainment tools. Mobile phones and tablets facilitate protégé learning and reflection and enable rapid mentoring conversations to ensue. These devices can enable mentors to provide feedback in more informed and objective ways (Hudson 64).

Mentoring tools must enable the mentor and protégé to accomplish learning and change in three key domains: *personal, experiential*, and *integrational*. First, the protégé must be able to acquire knowledge, skills, attitudes, and beliefs to enhance their personal performance. The protégé must also be able to apply these skills and gain confidence in their use through their daily experiences. Finally, the protégé must be able to assess outside sources of information, adopt new knowledge, and develop new practices informed by their personal and professional experiences.

Mentoring tools must also allow for reflection and evaluation of the protégé's development. The following are two mentoring innovations in the works:

E-mentoring, also known as "mobile computing platform learning" and "education in your palm," was an early development by researchers at FIU to provide opportunities for informal and formal education at any time and in any place. This was a peer-to-peer electronic mobile learning concept which could be used as a basis for future e-mentoring.

These systems enable the creation of knowledge outside the classroom, during afterschool programs, in community-based organizations, museums, libraries, and shopping malls, as well as the great outdoors in under-resourced settings (Nguyen). By designing, developing, and implementing context-aware, ubiquitous, self-directed learning methodologies through ad hoc sensor networks, these systems can interconnect and share information seamlessly.

Extending the concept of mobile education to mentoring, both mentors and protégés could develop interactions and relationships electronically, enabling mentorship to take place on-the-fly in any environment and at any time.

Location-based services for smartphones already provide incredible amounts of information based on our location, such as local restaurants, hotels, service stations, and shopping malls.

Situational-based mentoring, a new concept being researched in Germany, could provide on-the-spot mentors based on location and need, allowing protégés to tap into worldwide expertise on a variety of issues in wide-ranging locations, thus providing agility and flexibility in the mentoring process.

German researchers are also investigating another interesting concept: to employ chatbots as a tool to support one-on-one learning and mentoring experiences in higher education

(Neumann 1-7). They developed two chatbots known as FeedBot and LitBot to provide individual support for students' self-study.

Their systems were used specifically in dealing with seminar literature and in recommending study materials. The chatbots provided automated feedback and recommendations to their students, thereby reducing needed one-on-one interactions from mentors and teachers.

While the system worked well in supplementing support for the students, many students still expressed their desire to "talk to a real person" when difficulties arose. In assessing student feedback, Neumann et al wholeheartedly agreed with one student who stated: "I don't think that the bot is a replacement for personal discussions and interactions" (Neumann 6).

We agree. The system could, however, be used in the future to enrich interactions between students and mentors and provide a vehicle for a single mentor to be "on call" for multiple protégés, thereby increasing the range and flexibility for excellent mentors.

Remote Meeting Tools

In today's environment, mentoring via remote technology such as Zoom can enhance the mentoring relationship by providing rapid communications across international environments. When incorporating remote meeting tools, mentors and mentees can also employ a variety of AI tools for meetings to help capture key ideas during fast-paced, engaging sessions.

Another tool, Fireflies, is a meeting optimization tool using AI to transcribe, summarize, and analyze voice conversations. It can be incorporated in a variety of videoconferencing and cloud storage platforms and can connect to other applications via its application programming interface (API) (Davis). Transcriptions are searchable using keywords, themes, or conversation topics, as well as AI-based sentiment analysis.

A third such application is Duet AI for Google Workspace.

It uses AI to generate translated captions in 18 different languages, as well as providing notes and meeting summaries (ibid). Rather than missing a meeting, Duet AI could also be used to attend meetings as your proxy. The system can capture video snippets in real-time and provide latecomers to the meeting with a "summary so far" of the proceedings.

Virtual AI-generated simulations may also provide mentors and protégés tools for learning and feedback. SIMPROV, or simulated provocations, was developed by Arvola et al to provide teacher training students with common everyday scenarios for classroom situations. In this scenario, teachers were presented with text and images concerning the scenario and an introduction to describe the classroom situation followed by four distinct classroom leadership styles. The aim was to facilitate preservice teachers' knowledge development related to classroom management (Nesje 5; Arvola et al 98-114).

This and many other simulations could be readily adapted to mentoring scenarios in all fields, providing structured mentoring and experiential training.

Turning to Norway, researchers there are focusing on mentoring services hosted by digital mentoring platforms. Mentors and mentees in a study by Radlick et al identified a need for—

- connection,
- help in achieving goals, and the
- need for security and control

that could be implemented across digital platforms to better inform the mentoring process (1). Of these, connection, or a sense of community, was one of the overarching themes of the study. It incorporated the need for group activities as a way of socializing.

The authors identified the use of digital platforms as a way to enhance contact between the mentees and mentors. Mentees in the study emphasized that digital platforms should not take the place of human contact, "but rather supplement it." Many mentees also felt that existing "in person contact was too infrequent and that emotional bonding, showing empathy, and closeness could be challenging to facilitate remotely and would be preferable in person." (5).

The greatest concern both mentors and protégés expressed concerning digital platforms in mentoring is the need for security and control over their personal information.... Facebook and Instagram ... [were] identified ... as being unsafe.

The research also highlighted the need for social interaction with other people, particularly other groups of mentees which would allow more extensive development of social networks. Many organizations are finding the use of digital platforms to connect protégés with other protégés through associations with clubs to be an excellent source of social and emotional support. Current platforms being used for these interactions include WhatsApp group chats and other social media services.

The use of digital platforms can often blur or extend the distance in formal and informal mentoring relationships of mentor or friend. Radlik et al highlighted that some mentors slipped easily into an out of the informal role of friend for their protégés, while others "expressed concerns about intruding on their mentees personal spheres when using social media for communicating" (5).

The greatest concern both mentors and protégés expressed concerning digital platforms in mentoring is the need for security and control over their personal information (6). Depending on their familiarity with platforms such as Facebook and Instagram, protégés inevitably identified these platforms as being unsafe. Protégés had concerns about their anonymity, as well as their privacy when using different aspects of these platforms.

To provide better control for mentors and protégés alike, specific mentoring on advanced technologies may become an essential part of the mentoring experience.

MENTORING-THE-MENTOR IN ADVANCED TECHNOLOGY

In the age of *Mentoring Beyond AI*, mentors will need to be mentored on advanced mentoring techniques, as well as innovative technologies. Researchers are investigating several novel processes in education that can be applied to the mentoring of mentors. These include the development of digital access skills and technology integration.

Digital Technology

With the rapid pace of digital technology development, it is nearly impossible for mentors specialized in other areas to keep up with all the changes happening in the world around them. Even those in advanced technology fields find themselves racing to keep up with advances on multiple fronts. Each day new technologies are introduced into our society, and it seems that only younger members can rapidly acquire the skills and apply them to new applications and digital devices.

Digital access skills mentioned by René Hobbs as early as 2011 provided a warning concerning the acquisition of access skills for educators (Hobbs). Since that time, others have noted that digital and media literacy access is essential (Sevara et al) to interact with the current generation in any meaningful way.

Digital access, in many cases, will be media-specific, requiring familiarity with the media storage systems, as well as the specific computer or device used to access the media. This may require the development of numerous competencies outside of one's current expertise.

Human–machine interfaces (HMIs), commonly referred to as "dashboards," make it easier for a person to connect with a device or system allowing them to interact and access needed information more quickly.

> To provide better control for mentors and protégés alike, … advanced technologies may become an essential part of the mentoring experience.

A graphical user interface (GUI) allows humans to connect using graphical icons and visual indicators rather than text-based scripts to access information even more quickly with ease. However, the "ease" provided by these devices and systems is often in the eye of the developer more than the eye of the user, requiring some user training to unpack the full utility of the system.

One method proposed by Gusman Edouard to improve digital access skills and technology integration for educators is the application of *technology mentoring* (Edouard 124). This concept could easily be adapted and applied to the development of advanced technology acquisition for mentors. We will discuss this method in more detail in the next section.

Technology Mentoring

An interesting concept that has been advocated for use in colleges and universities is the concept of mentoring to maximize faculty technology integration efforts (Edouard 125). Beginning in 2022 with the Covid-19 pandemic, higher education has transitioned to more online courses requiring faculty members to use advanced technologies to teach.

Businesses have not been immune from these changes, as a wide variety of business activities are now being conducted in the digital workspace. Although advanced technology is becoming ubiquitous throughout our society, universities and businesses both find themselves in the unenviable position of struggling to *train* employees to incorporate and use these new technologies.

In 2006, Punya Mishra and Matthew Koehler introduced their Technological Pedagogical Content Knowledge framework, or TPACK, a system designed to understand and promote effective teaching with technology through three integrated types of knowledge: *technological knowledge* (TK), *pedagogical knowledge* (PK), and *technological pedagogical knowledge* (TPK) (24).

Roadblocks to technology integration include high time demand to learn and incorporate new technologies, current high workloads of employees, low salaries which reduce motivation for technology incorporation, and recurring technology issues upon implementation which incite the workforce to return to older methods of production (Lloyd 7).

CHALLENGES OF MENTORING IN THE AI AGE

Like any new technology, artificial intelligence has both benefits and disadvantages. In mentoring, both mentors and protégés must ensure that the use of artificial intelligence tools enhances, not decrements the mentoring relationship. Now and in the future, AI can provide faster communication and interaction outcomes, consistent results in improving a mentoring relationship across international divides and help us make smarter decisions.

But there are also many pitfalls in using AI tools. First and foremost, AI cannot provide a substitute for a solid *human* mentoring relationship. Mentoring is a human activity requiring the utmost care in developing one-on-one relationships between the mentor and protégé. AI can enhance our interactions and help us develop stronger relationships. It may also provide the mentor the capability of mentoring multiple protégés by reducing some of the time spent building the relationship.

There are specific technologies that are ubiquotous today we can discuss that have significant impact on our human relationships.

Chatbots and Other Robotics

Human-robot service interactions can pose some significant moral, ethical, and personal well-being implications. Many companies are now replacing human customer service representatives with chatbots, or personal assistants such as Alexa and Siri. Chatbots can also be used to conduct mentoring.

In an article in the Journal of Service Management titled, *Friend, mentor, lover: does chatbot engagement lead to psychological dependence?* Tianling Xie et al identified several interesting consequences of the use of the AI social chatbot Replika. The purpose of their study was to investigate "customer artificial intelligence service technology engagement and relationship development drivers, as well as potential negative consequences in the context of social chatbots" (806).

Over the years, advances in natural language processing have helped developers produce more humanlike chatbots. The beneficial effects of using social chatbots include the ability to form social-emotional relationships with consumers in a nearly human-compatible manner. However, these chatbots also come

with some potential strings attached. Social chatbots can introduce safety risks (Mahmood), as well as personal privacy and
security risks (Xie 806).

> AI cannot provide a substitute for a
> solid human mentoring relationship
> ...requiring ...one-on-one relationships
> between the mentor and protégé.

In their study, Xie et al identified that service robots are now
offering a broad array of services. As these devices more closely
emulate human characteristics, users sense that the bots are also
intuitive and compassionate, enabling users to form friendships
and romantic relationships with the bots (808).

Psychologists are identifying more and more instances of
consumers spending vast amounts of time with these technologies, negatively affecting users' mental and physical well-being
(Sherer 399). Xie's study revealed that in addition to the positive
values of customer well-being and improved mental health in
some respondents, a danger does exist in the use of these devices
and the potential negative consequences of device addiction
(Xie 822). They identified several study participants who became
deeply involved with (addicted to) the chatbots, as saying, "[it
was a] very intense experience" and "like a person whom I want
to be with 24-7" (Xie 813).

Generative AI Bias

AI also suffers from inherent bias of which even the developer
may not be aware. Software developers apply their thinking and
reasoning in the development of their algorithms which could be

biased. Generative AI cannot remove this bias, as there will be some bias in how the original AI "learned" from its data sets. If an error was baked in, ultimately it may come out.

If an AI application generates unexpected, incorrect outputs it can be said to be suffering from "hallucinations." AI hallucinations can prevaricate by generating irrelevant or nonsensical responses. Since AI applications format their responses based upon legitimate, learned data the answer might sound right yet be completely wrong.

For the unaware or uninitiated using the application to help make important decisions, the results could be disastrous. When using AI, it is best to remember the age-old computer wisdom, "garbage in – garbage out". Unless you are using a known, well-trained AI source, you have no idea how the system was trained to respond or whether the response you received is legitimate.

Legal Considerations

We are only now beginning to go through the legal considerations of AI. AI may expose the user to the risk of copyright infringement based on the AI prompt. And, as with anything digital, information placed in an AI application could be mined by a hacker with unscrupulous or malicious intent.

Laura Köbis and Caroline Mehner, professors at the Institute of Educational Sciences in Leipzig University, write, "Mentoring is a highly personal and individual process, in which mentees take advantage of expertise and experience to expand their knowledge and to achieve individual goals" (1). Within the existing cornucopia of laws and policies concerning the personal and individual mentoring process, the emergence of AI complicates the picture by introducing new laws and regulations, as well as data protection policies and guidelines.

In their recent work, Köbis and Mehner outline several ethical issues that must be addressed when using AI in mentoring, especially in secondary schools and universities. High on the list are the areas of privacy, surveillance, manipulation, opacity of AI systems, human-robot interaction, automation and employment, autonomous systems, machine ethics, artificial moral agents, and singularity (Köbis and Mehner; Müller).

■ ■ ■

KEY POINTS ABOUT ADVANCED TECHNOLOGY

We used this chapter to explore how technology has advanced and impacts mentoring, and to consider the challenges we can expect in the future. Following are key points to remember about rapidly evolving e-mentoring technologies:

1. A key concern about artificial intelligence is the potential for misuse as well as the intentional or unintentional bias that can be built into it during development.

2. Digital mentoring tools (e-mentoring) have been and continue to be created, using various digital devices and mobile telephones to link mentors and mentees accross distances.

3. The greatest concern that both mentors and mentees have expressed about e-mentoring platforms is the need for security and control over their personal information, and Facebook and Instagram were identified as unsafe.

4. The bottom line regarding advanced technologies is that AI cannot substitute one-on-one human relationships.

C H A P T E R

14

Mentoring in Virtual and Outer Space

Exploration is wired into our brains. If we can see
the horizon, we want to know what's beyond.

— Buzz Aldrin

THE THIRD INDUSTRIAL REVOLUTION gave us nuclear power, a technology that is, arguably, more threatening than beneficial. It is up to us—mentors and mentees—to assure AI technology, and the technologies that follow it, are beneficial for us and our posterity.

The newest age—the *Fourth Industrial Revolution* that began in this 21st Century to transform us from traditional manufacturing and industrial practices to a world integrated with digital technologies, artificial intelligence, robotics, the *Internet of Things* (IoT), and more—is taking humanity into *virtual space* and *outer space*.

The combination of the virtual and outer spaces is not just likely; it will help us meet others for mentoring "face to face," or explore "realistically" at unimaginable places, without leaving our homes—or earth. Or, might our posterity explore earth from their new colony on another celestial body?

THE METAVERSE AND MENTORING

In 2007 spatial computing entered the world of education in a big way. You may know the term "spatial computing" by its more popular term: the *metaverse*.

Initially conceived by MIT graduate researcher Simon Greenwold in 2003 to describe his work involving a combination of augmented reality prototypes, input devices that allow users to control computers through real-world actions, and three-dimentional (3-D) scanners, spatial computing spawned early work that eventually led to our present-day virtual reality, augmented reality, and mixed reality.

Spatial computing found its earliest use in the 1990s to describe techniques in the field of human-computer interaction primarily involving geographic information systems (GIS) and the human ability to interact with digital data, especially a 3-D environment, displaying geographic positions on the Earth and interacting with streets, buildings, and other urban areas and topographic projections.

The Metaverse Today

For mentoring purposes, the metaverse is still a two-dimensional web-based environment limited in providing full engagement and has negative impacts on students (Greenwold), such as—

- students' limited self-perception due to inadequate personalization of the learning experience,

- limited student participation, providing limited opportunities to participate and interact, and

- limited scope for teachers, trainers, and mentors to understand their audience and fully explain concepts due to both the digital media and the inability to assess students attention and engagement with the ideas being presented.

The metaverse is developing quickly, though, and today it is known as an amalgam of technologies hosted on the Internet that includes virtual reality, persistent virtual worlds, and augmented reality combining elements of the digital and physical worlds and whose resident space can be accessed through any digital device, including virtual/augmented reality glasses, personal computers, game consoles, cell phones and tablets (Ravenscraft). Through Internet access using a 3-D avatar, the metaverse provides games and entertainment, broad-ranging social engagement and interactions, access to the arts, online shopping, learning, and educational opportunities.

Through the use of holograms, participants in this new 3-D world can interact with those at a physical event, perhaps a night at the Sydney Symphony Orchestra, enjoying and discussing the performance late into the evening without ever leaving the farm in Des Moines, Iowa. Participants could be admiring clothing their friends are wearing, and near instantaneously order these items and have them delivered to their homes in time to wear them (at home) while their friends are wearing them in Sydney. We've already begun ordering food through applications and having it delivered in time to share a meal with our friends halfway around the world.

Key technology companies such as Microsoft, Meta, and Apple are entering the metaverse. With augmented reality glasses and headsets such as Apple's Vision Pro, whole new vistas are opening up in this world. Motion tracking tools can distinguish where people wearing the device are looking and incorporate hand movements to "interact physically" (digitally) in the 3-D world, which will allow exciting new interactions and human experiences. We already have sites on the Internet that allow the selection of clothing in virtual fitting rooms and the ability to move furniture inside our homes to see the exact size and fit of a particular sofa or dining room set.

In a recent study titled, "Meeting in the Metaverse: A New Paradigm for Scientific Mentorship," lead author Danny Radford shares his Cardiovascular Analytics Group experience incorporating mentorship activities in the metaverse (A59). Their group consisted of 86 members from 20 countries with 23 members participating in a metaverse experience (ibid).

An important factor in the study was that members of the group had a mean age of 28 years and approximately 28% of those in the study were female. The team used the metaverse for "delivery of teaching" within a healthcare environment.

Survey results focused on the metaverse and its" roles in facilitating virtual mentorship including accessibility, communication, and internationalization." Their results indicated that the metaverse "facilitated interactions with new members (72%) and helped facilitate interactions with members from other countries (67%) more than traditional video platforms alone" (ibid).

Group members also indicated the metaverse was "equally or more effective for teaching project related tasks." Respondents also highlighted their enjoyment in the *gamification* aspect of the metaverse (83%), while 73% of the respondents indicated that the metaverse platform facilitated mentorship (ibid).

A Future Metaverse for Education and Mentoring

The metaverse may provide an optimum platform for education and mentoring interactions. Online education has already become ubiquitous and very popular with both traditional and untraditional students. Massive Open Online Courses (MOOCS) attract large numbers of students from around the globe (Mitra 66). Educators are employing synchronous teaching-learning systems such as Microsoft Teams, Zoom, WebEx, and Skype to allow an online, virtual presence as well as interaction with the physical classroom setting.

Incorporation of the elements of the metaverse would allow an even more interactive presence for these students where, by using their avatar, the students would be actively interacting in the classroom rather than experiencing the ideas simply through a digital screen. We can discuss three of those elements now.

Three-dimensional metaverse tools. The previously discussed concepts of e-learning tools and mobile learning devices (M-learning) which provide an anywhere-at-any-time learning experience through the employment of digital devices, could be significantly enhanced with 3-D metaverse tools.

Mentors and educators can already provide cloud-based materials that international protégés and students could access via the cloud. However, the implementation of a 3-D metaverse environment using a virtual or augmented reality format could circumvent many of the problems previously discussed in the 2-D learning environment.

The metaverse could provide mentors with more opportunities for hands-on learning by, and assessment of, their protégés. By incorporating group activities, students could virtually immerse themselves as they do today in games with other protégés to increase social interactions and improve mentoring and learning outcomes.

Digital twins (DT), which are virtual representations or models of a physical object, system, or process, can accurately reflect real-world counterparts and enable interaction using sensors and existing data (IBM). The virtual models can be used to run simulations, conduct studies, and continue to generate valuable insights (ibid).

In the classroom, digital twins can be used to help visualize ideas and "concepts of the natural/physical world in metaverse-based education" making the learning experience more realistic, user-friendly, and immersive (Mitra 66). Digital twins are already being used in healthcare services to track health indicators and generate insights from patients.

Applications in mentoring could include digital twins to help explain new business processes, allow protégés to interact with hands-on concepts, or allow mentors and protégés to jointly see and understand long-term implications of changes in systems and processes. The digital twin's concept will provide immediate feedback and extraordinary opportunities for personal growth for both mentor and protégé.

Non-player characters. By incorporating artificial intelligence and machine learning (AI/ML), mentors can create automated virtual learning experiences and use the systems to assess progress and growth. Susanta Mitra suggests the development of *non-player characters* (NPC) within the metaverse to act as the protégés guides, answering frequently asked questions, evaluating their performance, and providing real-time feedback (70).

We are only now beginning to scratch the surface of potential uses for mobile-, hybrid-, and micro-learning environments within the metaverse. Studies have yet to be done on the use of the metaverse for educating children with special needs (Alam) and for gifted students.

Challenges in the Metaverse

One of the challenges for international mentoring using the metaverse is that the development and status of the metaverse differ from country to country based on government policies and attitudes, as well as markets in these countries.

From the standpoint of governments, use of the metaverse in each country can vary significantly. For example, in the United States, controls and regulators primarily focus on data security and privacy protection issues, and governments in the U.S. have implemented multiple laws to curb data misuse and privacy breaches by the public (Ning 14674).

On the other hand, China approaches this differently. In January 2022 China proposed a national policy for "forward-looking research and development to strengthen the basic capabilities of the underlying core technologies of the metaverse" (ibid). And control of the metaverse in China is through the China Mobile Communications Association Metaverse Consensus Circle that is directly under the control of the China Mobile Communications Association that is ultimately government-controlled, regulated, and restricted, as has been seen through recent controls of Internet access.

From the standpoint of governments, use of the metaverse in each country can vary significantly. For example, … the United States, …[has] implemented multiple laws to curb data misuse and privacy breaches by the public.… [C]ontrol of the metaverse in China … is ultimately government-controlled, regulated, and restricted.

In developing the metaverse, foundational technologies such as 5G and 6G telecommunications technologies form the bedrock for its use. To realize the full potential of the metaverse these technologies must provide high-speed, low latency, low power consumption, ubiquitous networks, and global interconnections (Ning 14677).

The Internet of Things will provide the network infrastructure for the metaverse, which will also require robust computing devices and will rely on improved cloud computing, edge computing, and improved capabilities beyond the scope of this book.

Users of the metaverse will be immersed in a virtual social world. This world will reflect real-world locations and interactions with a variety of user avatars interacting much as the real world in New York City or other large cities exist today. Shoppers, workers, tourists, and children will all form an interactive social network some of which may be known to a user and others may not.

Social privacy within the virtual social worlds of the metaverse will continue to be a challenge as users in the metaverse may be able to track and reveal the true identity of users and players, as well as their sensitive information, including location, shopping preferences, and financial information. Existing privacy controls may be insufficient in the metaverse due to the use of avatars and the ability of unknown avatars to track a user's personal records and information, track and understand a user's "visit history" to preferred locations and identify and steal other information.

Computer scientists and cybersecurity experts are actively working to develop privacy protection schemes within the metaverse. One idea being developed is disguising users by periodically changing the appearance of the avatar to make it more difficult for attackers to target specific individuals. In addition, some avatars could become "temporarily invisible" when being tracked (Ning 14682; Gogolin 30-42). More challenges will arise as our demands continuously outpace our technological developments.

On the dark side, the same graft, corruption, and crime that exists in the real world can and will be duplicated in the metaverse. It will of course be different than our current reality but will always be a part of the human condition. Those wishing to deprive others of their peace, prosperity, and happiness will continue to employ modern technologies to assault those around them to enrich their own lives.

Mentors will need to be even more aware of the technologies they employ, their potential for misuse, and the resulting negative outcomes on their protégés.

CHALLENGES OF MENTORING IN SPACE

We are sprinting through the gateway to the AI Age and beyond. There is no stopping, no slowing, nor turning back. We must harness the capabilities this new age of AI presents while maintaining that which is most precious, our ability to cultivate profound *human* relationships.

The expression "Space: the final frontier" has now given way to "Mentoring: Maintaining the Human Relationship in Space." As we employ AI tools to conquer international mentoring, we must now set our sights on interplanetary and, perhaps, intergalactic mentoring. How will we maintain the increasingly ubiquitous human connectivity as we forge our way into the frontiers of space?

Mentoring now and into the future will play an important role in overcoming barriers, promoting diversity in space travel, and building our future technologies. The tools we build today will be the foundations that encourage the next generation of space travelers. Roles and responsibilities will change to reflect the new technologies and needs of this new environment, but one thing will remain certain: mentoring will continue to be a necessary human activity in this new realm.

Over the last two decades, multiple international organizations have launched or are preparing to launch exploratory missions to Mars. This group has attempted experimental investigation and analysis of the Martian environment more than 55 times. Manned exploration of Mars has been the stated objective of several national efforts, including *Mars One*, a Swiss-Dutch effort that aims to establish a permanent human settlement on Mars (Kim).

[S]uppose mentoring was occurring between Earthbound mentors and Mars-bound astronauts on their long journey. If our communications were taking place at the speed of light through the vacuum of space ... [a]t their closest possible point, communications ... would be [delayed] approximately 3.03 minutes, while the furthest distance between the two would [would be delayed by] ... more than 22.4 minutes.

If we could start the rockets tomorrow to catapult us into space for a visit to Mars, NASA estimates that a one-way trip would take about nine months. The catch is for a return round-trip one would need to wait approximately three months on Mars to make sure Earth and Mars were in proper alignment for the return trip (Tillman). Overall, this 21-month trip would be a short stint compared to other extended space travel.

Now, suppose mentoring was occurring between Earthbound mentors and Mars-bound astronauts on their long journey. If our communications were taking place at the speed of light through the vacuum of space, we would nevertheless encounter some additional delay in the communication process. Since Earth and Mars are orbiting the sun in somewhat irregular patterns, the distance between the two planets is constantly changing (ibid). At their closest possible point, communications at the speed of light between the two planets would be approximately 3.03 minutes, while at the furthest distance between the two would require communication times of more than 22.4 minutes. Even using an average of 12.5 minutes per transmission would require a long mentoring interval.

New techniques and tools for learning, teaching, and mentoring will be required to compensate for the latency in telementoring in space and other challenges sure to be encountered in future manned space flight.

While some mentoring can be conducted long-term and with multiple practice iterations, some mentoring will require immediate interactions. In recent studies published in Aerospace Medicine and Human Performance, Tovy Kamine et al conducted evaluations simulating a surgical task requiring precision and accuracy for long-duration spaceflights. In their research, they set up an experiment using a simulated surgical task. Each of the surgical residents conducted two trials, one with a mentor in the same room and another with the mentor using a teleconference with time delays. Researchers measured the amount of time necessary to complete a task to successfully remove "game pieces," counted the number of errors, and recorded scores on the NASA task load index. Both the mentor and protégé were evaluated.

Results of the study indicated that residents in the time delay group experiencing only a 700-millisecond delay successfully removed far *fewer* pieces than those with the mentor co-located (Kamine). Interestingly, while scores for both groups indicated increased stress, it was the mentors who reported "significantly increased mental load," in working with their protégés under the time delay (ibid.).

New techniques and tools for learning, teaching, and mentoring will be required to compensate for the latency in telementoring in space and other challenges sure to be encountered in future manned space flight.

MENTORING IN A MATED METAVERSE AND SPACE

Researchers at the Institute for Creative Technologies, University of Southern California, Playa Vista, California and NASA Johnson Space Center in Houston, Texas, recently concluded a study on the use of virtual worlds for astronaut and ground crew training in preparation for long-duration spaceflights. The study concluded that virtual worlds offered a "promising technology for learning, preparing, and supporting long-duration spaceflight." (Morie.)

Since future astronauts will be part of the new "digital generation" that is "comfortable with learning, sharing, and socializing through technology," the authors of the study saw great benefit in adopting virtual worlds for learning (ibid). These same virtual worlds could be improved using AI and extended as tools for mentoring in space.

■ ■ ■

The information we have presented only begins to scratch the surface as we explore new concepts in *Mentoring in Virtual and Outer Space*. Many challenges and pitfalls lie before us. Nevertheless, we have every confidence these potential barriers will all be overcome in time if we remember the cardinal rule of mentoring:

Mentoring is a human activity
that builds and maintains a relationship
between mentor and protégé.

We hope the information presented in this book is informative and provides the reader with some of the skills and knowledge necessary to advance the mentoring relationship now and into the future.

Good mentoring!

Cited Works

Alam, Ashraf and Atasi Mohanty. "Metaverse and Posthuman Animated Avatars for Teaching-Learning Process: Interperception in Virtual Universe for Educational Transformation." *International Conference on Innovations in Intelligent Computing and Communications*, Springer, Cham, 2022.

Albion, Robert G. "The Communication Revolution, 1760-1933." *Transactions of the Newcomen Society*, vol. 14, no. 1, 1933, pp. 13-25.

Aristotle. *The Nicomachean Ethics.* Edited by Lesley Brown, translated by David Ross, Oxford World's Classics, Revised Edition, 2009.

Arvola, Mattias, et al. "Simulated Provocations: A Hypermedia Radio Theatre for Reflection on Classroom Management." *Simulation & Gaming*, vol. 49, no. 2, 2018, pp. 98-114.

Backstrom, Lars, et al. "Four Degrees of Separation." *Proceedings of the 4th Annual ACM Web Science Conference*, 2012.

Beatty, Alexandra, rapporteur. "Approaches to the Development of Character: Proceedings of a Workshop." *Board on Testing and Assessment, Division of Behavioral and Social Sciences and Education.* U.S. National Academies of Sciences, Engineering, and Medicine, National Academies Press, 2017.

Bell, A. W. "Diagnosing Students' Misconceptions." *The Australian Mathematics Teacher*, vol. 1, no. 1, 1982, pp. 6-10.

Bell, A. W. "Treating Students' Misconceptions." *The Australian Mathematics Teacher*, vol. 2, no. 1, 1982, pp. 11-13.

Berkowitz, Marvin, et al. "Effective Features and Practices that Support Character Development." Paper prepared for the *Workshop on Approaches to the Development of Character*, 26 July. The National Academies of Sciences, Engineering, and Medicine, Washington, D.C. December 2016, http://sites.nationalacademies.org/cs/groups/dbassesite/documents/webpage/dbasse_173494.pdf.

Berne, Eric. "Transactional Analysis: A New and Effective Method of Group Therapy." *Am. J. Psychother.*, vol. 12, 1958, pp. 735-743.

Besnoy, Kevin D., and Sara C. McDaniel. "Going Up in Dreams and Esteem: Cross-Age Mentoring to Promote Leadership Skills in High School–Age Gifted Students." *Gifted Child Today*, vol. 39, no. 1, 2016, pp. 18-30.

Brefi Group. "Coaching and Mentoring." http://www.brefigroup. co.uk/coaching/coaching_and_mentoring.html. Accessed 22 November 2017. Now https://threeticks.com/brefigroup.

Britannica Concise Encyclopedia. 2017.

Buckley, J., et al. "Defining and teaching evaluative thinking: Insights from research on critical thinking." *American Journal of Evaluation*, vol. 36, no. 3, 2015, pp. 375-388.

Busse, H., et al. "How Can Mentoring Programmes for Young People in Secondary Schools in the United Kingdom be Classified? Developing a Typology Using Qualitative Methods." *Journal of Epidemiology and Community Health*, vol. 71, no. A78, 2017.

Chase, W. G.. and H. A. Simon. "Perception in Chess." *Cognitive Psychology*, vol. 1, no. 1, 1973, pp. 33-81.

"CNBC Iconic Tour online." *CNBC*, 27 Sept. 2016, https://www. cnbc.com/2016/09/27/steve-jobs-advice-on-hiring-helps-grow-this-ceos-talent-pool.html.

Cognition and Technology Group at Vanderbilt. "From Visual Word Problems to Learning Communities: Changing Conceptions of Cognitive Research." 1994, pp. 157-200.

Cognition and Technology Group at Vanderbilt. "Classroom Lessons: Integrating Cognitive Theory and Classroom Practice." *Classroom Lessons: Integrating Cognitive Theory and Classroom Practice*, edited by K. McGilly, MIT Press/Bradford Books, 1997.

Committee on Developments in the Science of Learning with Additional Material from the Committee on Learning Research and Educational Practice, National Research Council. *How People Learn: Brain, Mind, Experience, and School: Expanded Edition*. National Academies Press, 2000. Dromgoole, Will Allen. "The Bridge Builder." Poetry Foundation, 1931. Accessed 24 November 2021.

Davis, Lee. "10 AI Tools in 2024." *Forbes Advisor*, https://www.forbes. com/advisor/business/ai-tools/.

De Groot, A. D. *Choice in Chess*. The Hague, Mouton, 1965.

Duckworth, Angela. *Grit: The Power of Passion and Perseverance*. Simon and Schuster, 2016.

Durlak, Joseph. "What You HAVE to Know about Program Implementation." Paper prepared for the Workshop on Approaches to the Development of Character," 26 July. *The National Academies of Sciences, Engineering, and Medicine*, Washington, DC. December 2016, http://sites.nationalacademies.org/cs/groups/dbassesite/documents/webpage/dbasse_173421.pdf.

Dweck, C. S. "Motivation." *Foundations for a Psychology of Education*, edited by A. Lesgold and R. Glaser, 87-136. Hillsdale, NJ: Erlbaum, 1989.

Edouard, Gusman. "Why and How Colleges and Universities Should Leverage Technology Mentoring to Maximize Faculty's Technology Integration Efforts." *TechTrends*, vol. 67, no. 1, 2023, pp. 124-132.

Eich, E. "Context, Memory, and Integrated Item/Context Imagery." *Journal of Experimental Psychology: Learning, Memory, and Cognition*, vol. 11, no. 4, 1985, pp. 764-770.

Erickson, Tim. "Using Simulation to Learn about Inference." Working Cooperatively in Statistics Education: Proceedings of the Seventh International Conference on Teaching Statistics, Salvador, Bahia, Brazil, 2006, pp. 2-7.

Ericsson, K. A., and H. A. Simon. *Protocol Analysis: Verbal Reports as Data*. MIT Press, 1993.

Erkut, Sumru, and Janice R. Mokros. "Professors as Models and Mentors for College Students." *American Educational Research Journal*, vol. 21, no. 2, 1984, pp. 399-417.

Evans, Nancy J., et al. *Student Development in College: Theory, Research, and Practice*. John Wiley & Sons, 2009.

Garringer, Michael, et al. "Policy and Procedure Manual Effective Strategies for Providing Quality Youth Mentoring In Schools and Communities." *The Hamilton Fish Institute on School and Community Violence* & The National Mentoring Center at Northwest Regional Educational Laboratory, Portland, 2008.

Graham, Alyssa. "Mentorship Functions and Educational Outcomes in Higher Education." 2022.

Glaser, R. "Expert Knowledge and Processes of Thinking." *Enhanc-*

ing Thinking Skills in the Sciences and Mathematics, edited by D. F. Halpern, Erlbaum, 1992, pp. 63-75.

Gleason, Nancy W. *Higher Education in the Era of the Fourth Industrial Revolution*. Springer Nature, 2018.

Gogolin, Greg, et al. "Virtual Worlds and social media." *International Journal of Artificial Life Research*, vol. 4, no. 1, Jan. 2014, pp. 30–42, https://doi.org/10.4018/ijalr.2014010103.

Gonsoulin Jr, Walter B., et al. "Learning by leading: Using best practices to develop leadership skills in at-risk and gifted populations." *Education*, vol. 126, no. 4, 2006, pp. 690-702.

Grassinger, R., et al. "Mentoring the gifted: A conceptual analysis." *High Ability Studies*, vol. 21, 2010, pp. 27-46.

Greenwold, Simon. "Spatial Computing." *Massachussetts Institute of Technology*, MIT, Master's Thesis, 2003.

Grossman, Jennifer Bowen, and Jean E. Rhodes. "The Test of Time: Predictors and Effects of Duration in Youth Mentoring Relationships." *American Journal of Community Psychology*, vol. 30, no. 2, 2002, pp. 199–219.

Guryan, Jonathan, et al. "The Effect of Mentoring on School Attendance and Academic Outcomes: A Randomized Evaluation of the Check & Connect Program." *Journal of Policy Analysis and Management*, vol. 40, no. 3, 2021, pp. 841-882.

Harrigan, Mark. "Transactional Analysis." *Disorders.Org*, 18 Oct. 2011, www.disorders.org/relationships/transactional-analysis/.

Hobbs, Renee. *Digital and Media Literacy: Connecting Culture and Classroom.* Corwin Press, 2011.

Howard, Nancy P. "A Brief History of Communications in the 18th Century." *18th Century History*, 2024, www.history1700s.com/index.php/articles/18-media/2591-a-brief-history-of-communications-in-the-18th-century.html. Accessed 27 January 2024.

Hudson, Peter. "Feedback consistencies and inconsistencies: Eight mentors' observations on one preservice teacher's lesson." European Journal of Teacher Education, vol. 37, no. 1, 2014, pp. 63-73.

IBM. "What is the digital twin." *IBM*, 2024, https://www.ibm.com/topics/what-is-a-digital-twin.

Ishiyama, J. "Expectations and Perceptions of Undergraduate Research Mentoring: Comparing First-Generation, Low-Income White/Caucasian and African American Students." *College Student Journal*, vol. 41, no. 3, 2007, pp. 540–549.

John Templeton Foundation. November 2016, www.templeton.org/what-wefund/core-funding-areas/character-virtue-development.

Johnson, W. Brad, and Charles R. Ridley. *The Elements of Mentoring*. 2004, ci.nii.ac.jp/ncid/BA69884132.

Kamine, Tovy Haber, Brandon W. Smith, and Gladys L. Fernandez. "Impact of Time Delay on Simulated Operative Video Tele-mentoring: A Pilot Study." *Aerospace Medicine and Human Performance*, vol. 93, no. 2, 2022, pp. 123-127.

Kim, David W. "Mars Space Exploration and Astronautical Religion in Human Research History: Psychological Countermeasures of Long-Term Astronauts." *Aerospace*, vol. 9, no. 12, 2022, p. 814.

Kohlberg, Lawrence, and Richard Mayer. "Development as the Aim of Education." *Harvard Educational Review*, vol. 42, no. 4, 1972, pp. 449-496.

Köbis, Laura, and Caroline Mehner. "Ethical Questions Raised by AI-Supported Mentoring in Higher Education." *Frontiers in Artificial Intelligence*, vol. 4, 2021, p. 624050.

Kraiger, K., et al. "Enacting Effective Mentoring Behaviors: Development and Initial Investigation of the Cuboid of Mentoring." *Journal of Business Psychology*, vol. 34, 2019, pp. 403-424.

Kupersmidt, Janis, et al. "Predictors of Premature Match Closure in Youth Mentoring Relationships." *American Journal of Community Psychology*, vol. 59, no. 1, 2017.

Lapsley, Daniel. *Moral Psychology*. Westview, 1996.

Larson, Reed. "Learning Character." Presentation prepared for the Workshop on Approaches to the Development of Character, 26 July. *The National Academies of Sciences, Engineering, and Medicine*, Washington, D.C. December 2016. http://sites.nationalacademies.org/cs/groups/dbassesite/documents/webpage/dbasse_173631.pdf.

Lesgold, A. M. "Acquiring Expertise." *Tutorials in Learning and Memory: Essays in Honor of Gordon Bower*, edited by J. R. Anderson and S. M. Kosslyn, Erlbaum, 1984, pp. 31-60.

Lesgold, A. M. "Problem Solving." *The Psychology of Human Thoughts*, edited by R. J. Sternberg and E. E. Smith, Cambridge University Press, 1988.

Lloyd, Steven A., Michelle M. Byrne, and Tami S. McCoy. "Faculty-Perceived Barriers of Online Education." *Journal of Online Learning and Teaching*, vol. 8, no. 1, 2012.

Mahmood, Syed H. "10 Virtual AI Companions to Chat and Have Fun With." *Make Use of (MUO)*, 24 September 2023, www.makeuseof.com/online-ai-chat-companions/.

Manning, Sandra, and Joanna Landrum. "An examination of Curricula Modifications Employed by Classroom Teachers for Intellectually Gifted Students in the General Education Classroom." The University of Southern Mississippi, 2005.

Marr, Bernard. "The Difference Between Generative AI And Traditional AI: An Easy Explanation For Anyone." *Forbes*, 24 July 2023, https://www.forbes.com/sites/bernardmarr/2023/07/24/the-difference-between-generative-ai-and-traditional-ai-an-easy-explanation-for-anyone/?sh=7ec6d969508a.

Marshall, Jim. "CommuniEGTcation Revolution of the 19th Century." *American History*, ABC-CLIO, 2019, americanhistory-abc-clio-pnw.orc.scoolaid.net/Search/Display/263201. Accessed 27 January 2024.

McCombs, B. L. "Alternative Perspectives for Motivation." *Developing Engaged Readers in School and Home Communities*, edited by L. Baker, P. Afflerback, and D. Reinking. Mahwah, NJ: Erlbaum, 1996, pp. 67-87.

McGrath, Ryan E. "Essential Virtues." Presentation prepared for the Workshop on Approaches to the Development of Character, 26 July. The National Academies of Sciences, Engineering, and Medicine, Washington, DC. December 2016, http://sites.nationalacademies.org/cs/groups/dbassesite/documents/webpage/dbasse_173629.pdf.

McQuillin, Samuel, et al. "Program Support and Value of Training in Mentors' Satisfaction and Anticipated Continuation of School-Based Mentoring Relationships." *Mentoring and Tutoring: Partnership in Learning*, vol. 23, 2015, pp. 133-148.

McQuillin, Samuel D., and Michael D. Lyons. "A National Study of Mentoring Program Characteristics and Premature Match

Closure: The Role of Program Training and Ongoing Support." *Prevention Science*, vol. 22, no. 3, 2021, pp. 334-344.

Milgram, Stanley. "The Small World Problem." *Psychology Today*, vol. 2, no. 1, 1967, pp. 60-67.

Miller, Andrew. "Best Practices for Formal Youth Mentoring." *The Blackwell Handbook of Mentoring: A Multiple Perspectives Approach.* Wiley-Blackwell, 2007, pp. 305-324.

Miller, G. A. "The Magical Number Seven, Plus or Minus Two. Some Limits on Our Capacity to Process Information." *Psychological Review*, vol. 63, no. 2, 1956, pp. 81-87.

Mirriam-Webster's Collegiate Dictionary, 11th ed, Merriam-Webster, 2014.

Mitchell, Melanie. *Artificial Intelligence: A Guide for Thinking Humans.* Farrar, Straus and Giroux, 2019.

Mishra, Punya, and Matthew J. Koehler. "Technological Pedagogical Content Knowledge: A Framework for Teacher Knowledge." *Teachers College Record*, vol. 108, no. 6, 2006, pp. 1017-1054.

Mitra, Susanta. "Metaverse: A Potential Virtual-Physical Ecosystem for Innovative Blended Education and Training." *Journal of Metaverse*, vol. 3, no. 1, 2023, pp. 66-72.

Morie, Jacquelyn Ford, et al. "Operational Assessment Recommendations: Current Potential and Advanced Research Directions for Virtual Worlds as Long-Duration Space Flight Countermeasures." *Interstellar Messaging: An Embodied Perspective* 2016, 2011.

Mukhopadhyay, Utpal. "Ramanujan's Circle: Inspirors, Patrons and Mentors." *Resonance*, vol. 19, no. 6, 2014, pp. 570-584.

Müller, V. C. "Ethics of Artificial Intelligence and Robotics." *The Stanford Encyclopedia of Philosophy*, edited by E. N. Zalta, 2020. Available at: https://plato.stanford.edu/archives/win2020/entries/ethics-ai/.

Nash, Ronald J. "The Active Mentor: Practical Strategies for Supporting New Teachers." Kiss Library, 2017. Abstract. Accessed from https://kisslibrary.com/book/A3B0161F988C25219DD5?utm_source=new-1510-reuse-a-2&utm_medium=banner&utm_campaign=newtraf&search=The+Active+Mentor%3A+Practical+Strategies+for+Supporting+New+Teachers&x=4744305.

Nesje, Katrine, and Eli Lejonberg. "Tools for the School-Based Mentoring of Pre-Service Teachers: A Scoping Review." *Teaching and Teacher Education*, vol. 111, 2022, p. 103609.

Neumann, Alexander Tobias, et al. "Chatbots as a Tool to Scale Mentoring Processes: Individually Supporting Self-Study in Higher Education." *Frontiers in Artificial Intelligence*, vol. 4, 2021.

Nguyen, Hien M. "Modeling, Designing, and Implementing an Ad-hoc M-Learning Platform that Integrates Sensory Data to Support Ubiquitous Learning." 2015.

NIAS-Maiya Prodigy Fellowship Programme. https://prodigy.net.in/nias-maiya-prodigy/96

Ning, Huansheng, et al. "A survey on the metaverse: The state-of-the-art, technologies, applications, and challenges." *IEEE Internet of Things Journal*, vol. 10, no. 16, 15 Aug. 2023, pp. 14671–14688, https://doi.org/10.1109/jiot.2023.3278329.

Nucci, Larry. "Character: A Multi-faceted Developmental System." Sites. nationalacademies.org/DBASSE/BOTA/DBASSE_171735, November 2016.

Ohio State University, Office of Human Resources, Learning and Development. "Mentoring Relationships." Gateway to Learning, https://gatewaytolearning.osu.edu/professional-career-development/taking-charge-your-development/mentoring/mentoring-relationships. Accessed 2017.

Parks, Sharon Daloz. *Big Questions, Worthy Dreams: Mentoring Young Adults in Their Search for Meaning, Purpose, and Faith.* Jossey-Bass, 2000, p. 135.

Penprase, Bryan Edward. "The Fourth Industrial Revolution and Higher Education." *Higher Education in the Era of the Fourth Industrial Revolution*, vol. 10, no. 1, 2018, pp. 978-981.

Phillips-Jones, Linda, et al. *100 Ideas to Use When Mentoring Youth: Activities and Conversations to Help Your Mentees Excel.* Mentoring Group, 2021. Available at https://mentoringgroup.com/books/100-Ideas-to-use-when-mentoring-youth.pdf.

Pintrich, P. R., and D. Schunk. *Motivation in Education: Theory, Research and Application.* Columbus, OH: Merrill Prentice-Hall, 1996.

Radford, Danny, et al. "Meeting in the Metaverse—A New Paradigm for Scientific Mentorship." *Heart*, 2022, pp. A59-A60.

Radlick, Rebecca Lynn, et al. "Experiences and Needs of Multicultural Youth and Their Mentors, and Implications for Digital Mentoring Platforms: Qualitative Exploratory Study." *JMIR Formative Research*, vol. 4, no. 2, 2020, p. e15500.

Rao, K. Srinivasa. "The Role of Mentors in the Life of the Mathematical Genius Srinivasa Ramanujan." *Journal of Ramanujan Society of Mathematics & Mathematical Sciences*, vol. 8, no. 2, 2021.

Ravenscraft, Eric. "What Is the Metaverse, Exactly?" *Wired*, Conde Nast, 15 June 2023, www.wired.com/story/what-is-the-metaverse/.

Rhodes, Jean. "Who Exactly Was Mentor?: A Stunning Revelation and Some Important Lessons." *The Chronicle of Evidence-Based Mentoring*, 6 June 2018, www.evidencebasedmentoring.org/who-was-mentor-a-stunning-revelation-with-important-lessons.

Russell, Stuart J., and Peter Norvig. *Artificial Intelligence: A Modern Approach*. London, 2010.

Sanchez, C., and A. Brown. "Science." American Association for the Advancement of Science, 2017.

Sevara, Shermamatova, Kholmatov Shakhriyor, and Abdulkhay Kosimov. "Implementation of Digital Tools in the EFL Classroom." *Online-Conferences* Platform, 2022.

Sherer, James, and Petros Levounis. "Technological Addictions." *Current Psychiatry Reports*, vol. 24, no. 9, 2022, pp. 399-406.

Simon, H. A. "On the Development of the Processes." *Information Processing in Children*, edited by S. Farnham-Diggory, Academic Press, 1972.

Simon, H. A. "Problem Solving and Education." *Problem Solving and Education: Issues in Teaching and Research*, edited by D. T. Tuma and R. Reif, Erlbaum, 1980, pp. 81-96.

Spencer, Renee, et al. "Breaking Up Is Hard to Do: A Qualitative Interview Study of How and Why Youth Mentoring Relationships End." *Youth & Society*, vol. 49, no. 4, 2017, pp. 438-460.

Spencer, Renée. "'It's Not What I Expected': A Qualitative Study of Youth Mentoring Relationship Failures." *Journal of Adolescent Research*, vol. 22, no. 4, 2007, pp. 331-354.

Stearns, Peter N. *The Industrial Revolution in World History*. Routledge, 2020.

Stromei, L. K. "Increasing Retention and Success Through Mentoring." *New Directions for Community Colleges*, vol. 2000, no. 112, 2000, pp. 55–62. https://doi.org/10.1002/cc.11205.

Suárez-Orozco, Carola. "The Role of Culture and Context on Character Development." Presentation prepared for the Workshop on Approaches to the Development of Character, 26 July. *The National Academies of Sciences, Engineering, and Medicine*, Washington, DC. December 2016, http://sites.nationalacademies.org/cs/groups/dbassesite/documents/webpage/dbasse_173633.pdf.

Talbert, J. E., and M. W. McLaughlin. "Understanding Teaching in Context." *Teaching for Understanding: Challenges for Policy and Practice*, edited by D. K. Cohen, M. W. McLaughlin, and J. E. Talbert. San Francisco: Jossey-Bass, 1993, pp. 167-206.

Tillman, Nola Taylor, and Daiy Dobrijevic. "How Long Does It Take to Get to Mars?" *Space.com*, https://www.space.com/24701-how-long-does-it-take-to-get-to-mars.html.

Trochim, William M., and Jennifer B. Urban. "Advancing Evaluation of Character Building Programs." Paper prepared for the Workshop on Approaches to the Development of Character, 26 July. *The National Academies of Sciences, Engineering, and Medicine*, Washington, D.C. December 2016, http://sites.nationalacademies.org/cs/groups/dbassesite/documents/webpage/dbasse_173497.pdf.

Turing, A. M. "Computing Machinery and Intelligence." *Mind*, vol. 59, no. 236, 1950, pp. 433-460.

Turner, Eric Gardner. "Greek Handwriting." *Britannica*, 2024, www.britannica.com/art/calligraphy/Byzantine-period.

Tysoe, John, and Allan Knott-Craig. *Connected: A Brief History of Global Telecommunications*. Bookstorm (Pty) Ltd., 2020.

Watson, John B. *Behaviorism*. Routledge, 2017.

Wavare, Mahesh S. "Srinivasa Ramanujan: A Genius Mathematician Since Antiquity." Available from https://www.shahucollegelatur.org.in/Research/Publications/2021-22/45.%20Mahesh%20Wavare.pdf

Wiley, Tonya, and Kate Schineller. "The Wisdom of Age: A Handbook for Mentors." *MENTOR*, 2015, http://www.mentoring.

org/new-site/wp-content/uploads/2015/09/Wisdom_of_
Age-A_Handbook_for_Mentors.pdf.

World Economic Forum. "Realizing Human Potential in the Fourth
Industrial Revolution: An Agenda for Leaders to Shape the
Future of Education, Gender and Work." *World Economic
Forum*, 2017.

Xie, Tianling, Iryna Pentina, and Tyler Hancock. "Friend, Mentor,
Lover: Does Chatbot Engagement Lead to Psychological
Dependence?." *Journal of Service Management*, 2023.

Youth.gov. "Benefits of Mentoring for Young People." *Youth.gov*,
https://youth.gov/youth-topics/mentoring/benefits-
mentoring-young-people.

Index

About the Authors

Jerry F. Miller, PhD, Colonel, USAF (Ret.)

Dr. Jerry F. Miller first served in the United States Air Force as a rescue/special operations helicopter pilot. He achieved the rank of colonel before retirement from the Air Force. In addition to being an evaluator pilot and squadron commander, he was also a resources, planning, and programming officer, deliberate plans officer, and foreign area officer for Latin America during his time in uniform. Upon leaving military service, he joined Florida International University (FIU) where he later earned his PhD in computer science. He learned the lesson of mentorship early, as a high school student, where he was too shy to ask for guidance. It cost him a scholarship. Since that time, he has been fortunate to have had mentors who recognized his potential and mentored him to success in academia as well. Today, he is actively mentoring computer science, cybersecurity, and information technology students, who will be our future leaders. More importantly, as we enter the age of artificial intelligence, Dr. Miller is mentoring more experienced mentors in the art and science of finding, connecting, and building lasting relationships with a new generation of protégés struggling to compete in our complex, rapidly changing technological world. Jerry lives in Miami, Florida, where he is married and has ample opportunity to practice mentoring in his blended, multicultural family of six children and their spouses, ten grandchildren, and two great-grandchildren.

Anitha Kurup, PhD

Dr. Anitha Kurup is a professor and the Head of the Education Program at the National Institute of Advanced Studies (NIAS), Bengaluru, India. She leads the National Gifted and Talented Education Program of the NIAS. The program was initiated by the office of the Principal Scientific Adviser of the Government of India in 2011. She and her team have developed Indian based identification protocols and mentoring mechanisms for the gifted children in India in the age group 3 to18 years for different populations: rural, urban, and aboriginal tribes. She has developed successful multi-stage multi-level mentoring models for the gifted children in India. Prof. Kurup was part of the National team that successfully advocated for the Education for the gifted and talented resulting in it's inclusion in the National Education Policy 2020 of India. Her research career spanning over two decades is marked by her passion and motivation to undertake research in critical areas, hitherto unexplored within the Indian subcontinent. The hallmark of her research career has been the innovation methodologies adopted for large scale research studies questioning existing theoretical frameworks to find solutions to the real-world problems. Thus, her contribution to research stands the test of time and has made critical contribution to the growth of the educational field in India.

S. Sitharama "Ram" Iyengar, PhD

Dr. S. S. "Ram" Iyengar is currently a Distinguished University Professor and a former Director of the Knight Foundation School of Computing and Information Sciences at FIU, Miami, Florida. He is also the founding director of the Discovery Lab, an undergraduate lab for mentoring students in research. Prior to joining FIU, Dr. Iyengar was Roy Paul Daniel's Distinguished Professor and Chairman of the Computer Science department at Louisiana State University for over 20 years. During the last four decades, he has supervised and mentored over 55 Ph.D. students, more than 100 Master's students, and many undergraduate students who are now faculty at major universities worldwide, as well as scientists or engineers at national labs and industries around the world. He has published more than 500 research papers, and authored, co-authored, or edited 22 books. Dr. Iyengar is a member of the European Academy of Sciences, a Fellow of the Institute of Electrical and Electronics Engineers (IEEE), the Association of Computing Machinery (ACM), the American Association for the Advancement of Science (AAAS), the Society for Design and Process Science (SDPS), the National Academy of Inventors (NAI) and the American Institute of Medical and Biological Engineering (AIMBE).

Niki Pissinou, PhD

Dr. Niki Pissinou, a professor and the Director of the FIU Tele-communications and Information Technology Institute, has been a champion of mentoring women and underrepresented groups in STEM throughout her active professional career. She has published over two hundred and fifty research papers in peer-reviewed journals, conference proceedings, and book chapters on her specialty areas of computer networking, telecommunications, distributed systems, mobile computing, security, and aspects of nontraditional data management. She has also co-edited over four texts in the areas of mobile and wireless networking and systems and over fourteen IEEE and ACM conference volumes. Widely cited in books and research papers, her research has been funded by NSF, DHS, NASA, DOT, DoD, state governments, and industry. She has graduated over nineteen Ph.D. students who now hold positions in academia, federal government, and industry, and has mentored countless other graduate and undergraduate students, as well as faculty.

Naveen Kumar Chaudhary, PhD

Dr. Naveen Kumar Chaudhary has been a professor of Cyber Security at the National Forensic Sciences University in Gandhinagar, Gujarat, India since 2019. He is also a Courtesy Research Professor at the Knight Foundation School of Computing and Information Sciences at Florida International University, Miami, Florida. He holds a Bachelor of Technology degree in Information Technology & Telecommunication Engineering and Master of Engineering degree in Digital Communication. He earned his Ph.D. in Engineering and advanced certifications in Cyber and Network security. His extensive experience spans more than 25 years in engineering education, research, and government. He has steered many cutting-edge ICT projects and worked extensively on policy formulation in cybersecurity and e-governance. He is the recipient of a letter of appreciation for contribution towards the cause of literacy from Brent St. Denis, MP, Algoma Canada, in 1994. Dubai, SEWA award for his contribution to Cyber Security education in 2022. He also received COAS and CCOSC Commendation in 2009 and 2015, respectively for his innovation and distinguished service. He is an IEEE senior member and life member of IETE

www.ingramcontent.com/pod-product-compliance
Lightning Source LLC
Chambersburg PA
CBHW072100040426
42334CB00041B/1516